本套教材出版获以下资助：

暨南大学高水平大学建设专项资金

教育部中外语言交流合作中心国际中文教育精品教材“1＋2”资助工程

CENTER FOR LANGUAGE EDUCATION AND COOPERATION
中外语言交流合作中心

国际中文教育精品教材

暨南大学华文学院
College of Chinese Language and Culture, Jinan University

汉语言专业规划系列教材

MULTIMEDIA PRINT READER
MPR
www.mpreader.com

i学中文

第四册

总主编◎王衍军　林奕高　张　艳

分册主编◎王　辰　童盛强

暨南大学出版社
JINAN UNIVERSITY PRESS

中国·广州

图书在版编目（CIP）数据

i 学中文. 第四册 / 王衍军，林奕高，张艳总主编；王辰，童盛强分册主编. —广州：暨南大学出版社，2024. 11
汉语言专业规划系列教材
ISBN 978-7-5668-3866-7

Ⅰ. ①i… Ⅱ. ①王… ②林… ③张… ④王… ⑤童… Ⅲ. ①汉语—对外汉语教学—教材 Ⅳ. ①H195. 4

中国国家版本馆 CIP 数据核字（2023）第 247140 号

i 学中文（第四册）
i XUE ZHONGWEN（DI-SI CE）
总 主 编：王衍军 林奕高 张 艳
分册主编：王 辰 童盛强

出 版 人：阳 翼
项目统筹：杜小陆
责任编辑：张 钊
责任校对：刘舜怡 陈慧妍
责任印制：周一丹 郑玉婷

出版发行：暨南大学出版社（511434）
电 话：总编室（8620）31105261
营销部（8620）37331682 37331689
传 真：（8620）31105289（办公室） 37331684（营销部）
网 址：http：//www. jnupress. com
排 版：广州良弓广告有限公司
印 刷：广州市金骏彩色印务有限公司
开 本：787mm×1092mm 1/16
印 张：17. 75
字 数：220 千
版 次：2024 年 11 月第 1 版
印 次：2024 年 11 月第 1 次
定 价：68. 00 元

前　言

本套教材是面向非华裔初级中文学习者的综合教材。编者们根据学习对象的特点，结合来华留学生日常生活交际需求，选取反映当代中国社会生活、经济、科技等方面的相关内容，利用融媒体等新技术，以独特的视角向学习者展示了真实的当代中国社会。

本套教材分为六册，共71篇课文，其中第一册15篇，第二、三、四册各12篇，第五、六册各10篇。教材内容从零起点开始，可满足初级到准中级阶段学生中文学习的需要，教师可根据学生水平和课时安排选择相应的册数和课文。整体上看，教材内容难度呈螺旋上升形态，其中，第一、二册侧重HSK一、二级水平，第三、四册侧重HSK三、四级水平，第五、六册侧重HSK五、六级水平。

除了纸质版教材外，我们还制作了配套的数字化教材、课件、语言点讲解视频、录音材料、Quizlet词卡。数字化教材除了呈现纸质版教材的生词、课文及语言点外，还配备了生词和课文的录音、生词的例句或图片讲解，以及与纸质版教材不同的练习题和测试题，为学习者预习与复习提供更丰富的形式和内容，方便学习者更有效地利用碎片化时间进行学习，从而让“课前—课堂—课后”形成更紧密的有机整体。

本套教材突出“新”和“活”的特色。“新”主要体现在两个方面：一是课文内容选材新。如微信、“双十一”、快递、外卖、移动支付等都是与当代中国人生活密切相关的主题。二是练习形式新。如设计了利用智能语音识别完成的题型，以及制作上传至社交账号上的视频作业；在数字化教材上实现听写、配对、组句等多样化的练习题型；在课堂练习部分，围绕教学重点内容提供了一些游戏、比赛、情景扮演类练习，互动性强，能活跃课堂气氛，增强学习的趣味性。“活”主要体现在强调学生对所学内容要活学活用，充分利用学生在中国学习的语言环境，设计实践性、交际性任务，推动学生从课堂走到课外，通过完成相关任务，克服畏惧心理，达到多用中文、敢用中文、会用中文的学习效果。

一、教材使用说明

1. 教学目标

本套教材内容编写以功能为导向，以任务型和交际型为主线，结合现代信息科学技术，通过大量听、说、读、写训练，培养学习者基本的中文交际能力；通过语言实践与互动，培养学习者得体的语言交际能力。

2. 适用对象

本套教材的适用对象为零起点的初级到准中级水平中文学习者。六册教材总学习时长为 2 年左右，每周学习 10 ~ 12 课时（每课时 45 ~ 50 分钟）。

3. 教材体例

本套教材的体例是：课前热身—生词—课文—语言知识—练习。“课文”从交际需求、感兴趣话题、热点话题角度进行编写。“练习”涵盖生词、语言知识、交际、课堂活动、实践拓展等内容，其中大部分内容可在课上与学生一起完成。还有一些练习需要学生课下进行语言实践，凸显交际性。教师可以根据情况选用各类练习。

4. 教材使用建议

各册教学课时安排：

拼音部分：16～20课时。

第一、二、三册：6～8课时/课。

第四、五、六册：8～10课时/课。

拼音部分建议集中教学。课堂游戏或活动部分，教师可以根据需要进行选择。语音、汉字的教学始终贯穿教材。每册都有一些只要求识记、不要求书写的认读字。遵循循序渐进、由易到难的教学原则。

5. 配套资料说明

本书生词和课文配有录音，音频文件请在暨南大学出版社官网（http://www.jnupress.com）下载专区免费获取。Quizlet词卡，请在Quizlet官网（https://quizlet.com/join/Zmf6k5NtM?i=28qrwz&x=1bqt）"暨南大学i学中文教材"处获取。微课视频，书中标有"教学视频"标志，请扫码查看。

二、特别说明

教材编写人员尊重所有图片、肖像的知识产权。教材中所使用的图片大多来源于"熊猫办公"网站。编写团队已购买"熊猫办公企业VIP至尊版（ID：47206601）"图片下载和使用权限，并获取了每一张图片的版权使用协议。熊猫办公企业VIP至尊版权限明确标注：图片可用于"图书出版：报纸配图、杂志封面及配图、图书封面及配图"，编写团队也保证所下载图片仅用于本套教材及其配套资源的出版和教学，不作他用。

教材中有一些照片由我们的同事及留学生等出镜拍摄并友情提供，均授权我们在教材中使用，对此表示衷心的谢意。此外，本套教材中还有极少量的图片我们未能及时联络上作者，在此也希望图片作者联络我们，以便及时支付相应图片稿酬。

在编写过程中，我们也参考了其他教材、词典等书籍以及网络资料，我们尊重各位作者的知识产权，在此也表示真诚的感谢。

教材录音团队是普通话一级甲等的资深播音员陆圆圆和何浩源，他们有着丰富的宣传片、纪录片、广告片等的录音经验和主持经验。

教材封面图片来源于雕塑家廖慧兰女士为暨南大学华文学院特别创作的雕塑作品《五洲学子》，现竖立于暨南大学华文学院南门。廖慧兰教授的女儿、资深艺术媒体人及策展人曹丹给予了支持。对此我们表示感谢。

教材编写是一项极其复杂、艰巨的任务。本套教材的编者都为富有教学经验的一线中文教师，团队群策群力，收集整理了众多资料，在编写工作中投入了大量的精力和时间。初稿完成后经过多次试用，并根据专家学者、试用教师和学习者的意见进行了反复修改。在此，再次对为本套教材写作、出版等付出辛劳的专家、教师、编辑、学生等表示由衷的感谢！然而，由于编者能力和水平有限，教材难免存在疏漏，恳请各位教材使用者提出宝贵建议，以便在下次修订时进一步完善和提高。

教材编写组

2024 年 3 月

Preface

This set of textbooks is designed for beginner-level learners of Chinese who are not of Chinese descent. According to the characteristics of the learners, combined with the daily communication needs of international students in China, the editors selected relevant content reflecting contemporary Chinese social life, the economy, science and technology, and used new technologies such as multimedia to show the modern side of Chinese society to learners from a unique perspective.

This series consists of six volumes, containing a total of 71 texts: 15 texts in the first volume, 12 texts in each of the second, third, and fourth volumes, and 10 texts in each of the fifth and sixth volumes. The textbook starts at a beginner level with no prior knowledge required and progresses to an intermediate level. Teachers can select texts based on the students' level. The textbook in this series present different levels of difficulty, among which volumes one and two will focus on HSK levels 1 and 2, volumes three and four will focus on HSK levels 3 and 4, and volumes five and six will focus on HSK levels 5 and 6.

In addition to paperback textbooks, digital textbooks, courseware, language guidelines explanation video, recording materials, Quizlet word card have also been created. In addition to presenting new words, texts, and language guidelines of paperback textbooks, digital textbooks are also equipped with audio recordings of new words and texts, explanation of example sentences or pictures of new words and texts, as well as exercises and tests that are different from those in the paperback textbooks, which provide a wider range of options for learners to preview and review content, allowing them to make better use of their study time. So that it may smooth out the process of previewing before the class, learning within the classroom, and reviewing after the class to form an organically cohesive learning experience.

This series of textbooks emphasizes the features of being new and dynamic. The newness is mainly reflected in two aspects: First, the selected topics are new. Such examples include WeChat, "Double Eleven", express delivery, takeout, mobile payment, which are closely related to modern Chinese people's lives. Second, the method of practice is also new. For example, in the exercises, questions were designed to be completed by automatic speech recognition, and video assignments that can then be posted to social accounts. The digital teaching materials also have dedicated sections for dictation, matching, sentence making, and other diversified types of exercises types. The classroom practice, games, competitions, and scenarios around the key contents are provided, and they have been designed to be highly interactive to increase student engagement. The dynamism is mainly reflected in the emphasis that students should learn to use their own methods of learning to make full use of the language environment in which students can learn in China, thus practical and communication tasks have a heavy emphasis on skills that enable students to better put knowledge obtained from class into practice. By completing relevant tasks, students can overcome their fear and achieve the desired learning effect of using Chinese more frequently and boldly, knowing how to use Chinese in their everyday lives.

Instruction for teaching materials

Teaching objective

These textbooks are designed with a focus on function, task-based learning, and communication. These textbooks integrate modern information science and technology, providing extensive practice in listening, speaking, reading, and writing. This approach aims to develop learners' basic communication skills in Chinese, while enhancing their ability to interact in a socially appropriate manner.

Applicable object

This series is designed for beginner with no prior knowledge of Chinese to intermediate learners. The total learning duration for the six volumes is approximately 2 years, with a recommended weekly study load of 10 to 12 class hours (each class hour lasting 45 – 50 minutes).

Textbook structure

The structure of these textbooks is: Warming up, New Words, Text, Language Guidelines, Exercises. The texts are written from the perspective of the needs that arise from communication, topics of interest, and trending topics. Exercises cover new words, language guidelines, communication tasks, classroom activities, practical application tasks, and more. Most of these can be completed in class with students. In particular, there are some exercises that require students to carry out language practice after class to highlight the communicative nature. Teachers can choose various exercises according to the situation.

Suggestions for use

Schedule of teaching hours for each volume:

The Pinyin part: 16 – 20 class hours.

Books 1, 2, and 3: 6 – 8 hours per lesson.

Books 4, 5, and 6: 8 – 10 hours per lesson.

The Pinyin section should be taught intensively. Classroom games and activities can be chosen by the teacher according to their needs. The teaching of pronunciation and Chinese characters is embedded throughout the textbook. Each volume has a number of characters that are only required to be memorized, not written. The teachers should follow the principle of gradual progression from easy to difficult.

Description of Supporting Materials

This book includes audio recordings for new words and texts, which can be downloaded for free from the Jinan University Press official website (http://www.jnupress.com) in the download section. Quizlet flashcards can be accessed on the Quizlet website at https://quizlet.com/join/Zmf6k5NtM?i=28qrwz&x=1bqt under "Jinan University iLearn Chinese Textbook". Micro-lesson videos, marked with the "Teaching Video" symbol in the book, can be viewed by scanning the chain code.

Special Note

We would like to stress that our textbook compilation team respects the copyright of pictures and portraits, and the sources of the textbook materials are indicated where applicable. Most of the pictures used in the textbook were downloaded from the website "Panda Office". The compilation team has purchased the "Panda Office Enterprise VIP Supreme Edition (ID: 47206601)" and has fair use policy for use of its pictures stipulated in the user agreement section after purchase. "Panda Office Enterprise VIP Supreme Edition" clearly indicates the permission that pictures can be used for "book publication: newspaper illustrations, magazine covers and illustrations, book covers and illustrations". Our team also guarantees that the downloaded pictures will only be used for the publication and teaching of books and textbook companion resources (digital and paperback), and will not be used for other purposes.

Some photos in the textbook were taken by our colleagues and international students, who have kindly granted us permission to use these images in the textbook, for which we express our heartfelt gratitude. In addition, there are a small number of images in the textbook for which we were unable to contact the authors in time. We kindly request that the image authors reach out to us so that we can arrange payment for the corresponding image royalties.

In the process of writing this textbook, reference to other textbooks, dictionaries and other books as well as online materials was made. We respect the intellectual property rights of all authors and hereby express our sincere thanks.

The textbook recording team consists of senior announcers for first-level Mandarin proficiency, namely Lu Yuanyuan and He Haoyuan. They possess extensive experience in recording promotional videos, documentaries, commercials, and have experience in hosting as well.

On the textbook cover is a photo of the sculpture *Students from All*

Corners of the World, which stands at the south gate of the College of Chinese Language and Culture, Jinan University. As a special gift for the college, it was designed and created by Liao Huilan, a renowned sculptor in China. Heartfelt thanks go to Prof. Liao's daughter Cao Dan, a senior art journalist and exhibition curator, for her efforts in granting copyright authorization.

The compilation of textbooks is an extremely complex and arduous task. The editors are all front-line Chinese teachers with diverse teaching experiences, who gathered and sorted out the materials, and invested a lot of energy and time in the compilation of the collected work. After the submission of the first draft, the textbooks have undergone multiple revisions in rounds of trials, with the opinions of experts and scholars taken into consideration. Once again, we expressed our heartfelt thanks to the experts, teachers, editors, and students who have worked hard on the writing and publication of this book. However, due to the limited ability and skills of the editors, there were inevitable situations that omissions in the teaching materials occurred, and we sincerely hope that all the users of the textbooks can provide valuable suggestions for further improvement in the next revision.

The Compilation Team of the Textbook

Mar., 2024

人物简介

Character Introduction

林一 Lín Yī
性别：男
国籍：中国

王乐乐 Wáng Lèle
性别：女
国籍：中国

阿里 Ālǐ
性别：男
国籍：美国

米亚 Mǐyà
性别：女
国籍：法国

米娜 Mǐnà
性别：女
国籍：埃及

艾文 Àiwén
性别：男
国籍：德国

安娜 Ānnà
性别：女
国籍：英国

中文词类简称表

Abbreviations of Word Classes

1	名词	míngcí	名	noun
2	代词	dàicí	代	pronoun
3	动词	dòngcí	动	verb
	离合词	líhécí		separable verb
4	形容词	xíngróngcí	形	adjective
5	数词	shùcí	数	numeral
6	量词	liàngcí	量	measure word
	数量词	shùliàngcí	数量	numeral-classifier compound
7	副词	fùcí	副	adverb
8	介词	jiècí	介	preposition
9	连词	liáncí	连	conjunction
10	助词	zhùcí	助	particle
	动态助词	dòngtài zhùcí		aspect particle
	结构助词	jiégòu zhùcí		structural particle
	语气助词	yǔqì zhùcí		modal particle
11	叹词	tàncí	叹	interjection
12	象声词	xiàngshēngcí	象	onomatopoeia
13	前缀	qiánzhuì		prefix
14	后缀	hòuzhuì		suffix

目　录

Contents

前　言　/001

Preface　/005

第一课　你带钱包了吗 Do you have your wallet　/001

课前热身 Warming up　/001

生词 New words　/001

课文 Text　/004

语言知识 Language guidelines　/006

知识 1　“从”　/006

知识 2　“弄”　/007

知识 3　“其他”　/009

知识 4　“甚至”　/010

知识 5　“随着”　/012

练习 Exercises　/013

第二课　出门靠朋友 Rely on friends when you go out　/019

课前热身 Warming up　/019

生词 New words　/019

课文 Text /021

语言知识 Language guidelines /023

知识 1 “靠” /023

知识 2 “一……就……” /024

知识 3 “一切” /024

知识 4 “恨不得” /026

练习 Exercises /027

第三课 我的脚扭伤了 I sprained my foot /032

课前热身 Warming up /032

生词 New words /032

课文 Text /034

语言知识 Language guidelines /036

知识 1 “都……了” /036

知识 2 “……得厉害” /036

知识 3 “结果” /037

知识 4 “还” /037

练习 Exercises /038

第四课 租房 Rent a house /045

课前热身 Warming up /045

生词 New words /045

课文 Text /048

语言知识 Language guidelines /049

知识 1 “算” /049

知识 2 “不是……，就是……” /050

知识 3 “可” /051

知识 4 存现句 /053

知识 5 “更不用说” /054

练习 Exercises /055

第五课 中国的高铁真方便 China's high-speed rail is so convenient /062

课前热身 Warming up /062

生词 New words /062

课文 Text /064

语言知识 Language guidelines /066

知识 1 “了不起” /066

知识 2 “另外” /066

知识 3 “刚好” /067

练习 Exercises /068

第六课 坐飞机 Take a plane /075

课前热身 Warming up /075

生词 New words /075

课文 Text /078

语言知识 Language guidelines /080

知识 1 “把”字句$_1$ /080

知识 2 “忽然” /081

知识 3 “由于” /082

知识 4 “临时” /084

知识 5 “透了” /084
练习 Exercises /085

第七课 学做中国菜 Learn to make Chinese food /094
课前热身 Warming up /094
生词 New words /094
课文 Text /097
语言知识 Language guidelines /098
知识 1 “干” /098
知识 2 “接着” /100
知识 3 “把”字句$_2$ /101
知识 4 “于是” /104
知识 5 “到底” /105
练习 Exercises /106

第八课 又到“双十一” It's double 11 again /114
课前热身 Warming up /114
生词 New words /114
课文 Text /117
语言知识 Language guidelines /118
知识 1 “被”字句 /118
知识 2 “只有……才……” /120
知识 3 “……是……，不过/但是……” /122
知识 4 “各” /123
知识 5 “着” /125

练习 Exercises /126

第九课 送货上门 Home delivery /134

课前热身 Warming up /134

生词 New words /134

课文 Text /137

语言知识 Language guidelines /138

知识 1 “连……也/都……” /138

知识 2 “许多” /139

知识 3 “立刻” /141

知识 4 “无论……，都/也……” /142

知识 5 “不是……而是……” /144

练习 Exercises /145

第十课 减肥 Lose weight /153

课前热身 Warming up /153

生词 New words /153

课文 Text /155

语言知识 Language guidelines /157

知识 1 “终于” /157

知识 2 “又 + 不/没” /159

知识 3 “再说” /160

知识 4 趋向补语的引申用法 /161

知识 5 “竟然” /168

练习 Exercises /169

第十一课　我办了张健身卡 I got a gym membership　/178

课前热身 Warming up　/178

生词 New words　/178

课文 Text　/181

语言知识 Language guidelines　/182

知识 1　“……的话”　/182

知识 2　“恰好”　/183

知识 3　“就是”　/185

知识 4　“趁着”　/185

知识 5　“尽管……，还是/但是/可是……”　/186

练习 Exercises　/188

第十二课　你看足球比赛吗 Do you watch the football match　/196

课前热身 Warming up　/196

生词 New words　/196

课文 Text　/199

语言知识 Language guidelines　/200

知识 1　“一连”　/200

知识 2　“反正”　/201

知识 3　“有着”　/202

知识 4　“受到”　/203

练习 Exercises　/204

参考答案 Answers　/210

词汇表 Vocabulary　/243

第一课　你带钱包了吗

Do you have your wallet

课前热身 Warming up

你知道怎么用手机付款吗？你觉得用手机付款有什么好处和坏处？

Do you know how to pay by cell phones? What do you think the advantages and disadvantages of paying by cell phones are?

生词 New words

1	钱包	qiánbāo	名	wallet
2	便利店	biànlìdiàn	名	convenience store

3	啦*	la	助	the combination of "了" and "啊", indicating the tone of exclamation and doubt
4	弄	nòng	动	play with; fool with; to do, to handle
5	绑定	bǎng dìng		to bind
6	零钱	língqián	名	pocket money; small change
7	首页	shǒu yè		home page
8	角	jiǎo	名	horn; angle; corner
9	加号	jiā hào		plus sign
10	设置	shèzhì	动	to set up; to put up; to install; to fit
11	付款	fù kuǎn		to pay a sum of money
12	简单	jiǎndān	形	simple; uncomplicated
13	成为	chéngwéi	动	to become; to turn into
14	十分	shífēn	副	very; fully
15	不仅……还……	bùjǐn……hái……		not only...but also...
16	工具	gōngjù	名	tool; means; instrument
17	其他	qítā	代	the other

说明：加＊的词语不要求掌握书写。

Note: Competence in writing words marked with asterisk is not required.

18	功能	gōngnéng	名	function
19	其中	qízhōng	名	in；among
20	值得一提	zhídé yì tí		it is worth mentioning
	值得	zhídé	动	to be worth；to deserve
	提	tí	动	to carry (in one's hand with the arm down)；lift；raise；promote；to mention；to bring up
21	比如	bǐrú	动	for example；such as
22	甚至	shènzhì	连	even
23	摊	tān	名/动	booth；stall；spread out
24	煎饼*	jiānbing	名	thin pancake made of millet flour，etc.
25	话费	huàfèi	名	phone bill
26	水电费	shuǐ diàn fèi		water and power bills
	电	diàn	名	electricity；power
27	营业厅	yíngyè tīng		service hall；business hall
	营业	yíngyè	动	to do business；to open
	厅	tīng	名	hall
28	转账	zhuǎnzhàng	动	to transfer money (to a bank account)
29	办理	bànlǐ	动	to handle；to deal with；to conduct

30	动	dòng	动	to move; to stir; to act; to get moving
31	完成	wánchéng	动	to complete; to finish
32	随着	suízhe	介	along with; in the wake of
33	技术	jìshù	名	technology; skill; technique

课文 Text

课文1 Text 1

（林一和阿里在一家便利店，选完东西，准备付钱。）

林一：怎么啦？

阿里：哎呀，我忘记带钱包了，怎么办？

林一：没事儿，现在中国很多店都支持手机支付，你可以用手机来付钱。

阿里：可我从没用过手机付钱，要怎么弄？

林一：你有微信或者支付宝吗？

阿里：我有微信，然后呢？

林一：如果你的微信绑定过银行卡，或者微信钱包里有零钱，就可以。

阿里：我的微信钱包里好像有20多块钱，是在班群里抢红包抢到的。

林一：那就行了，你打开微信，在微信首页的右上角有一个加号，打开，然后选择“扫一扫”，就可以扫桌上的二维码了。

阿里：是吗？我试试。

林一：对了，第一次用，应该要先设置一下付款密码。

…………

阿里：弄好了。我来扫一下。

(微信支付15元！)

林一：你看，就是这么简单！

阿里：太方便了，以后出门我就不带钱包啦！

课文2 Text 2

现在，手机已经成为人们生活中十分重要的伙伴。它不仅是人们用来联系的工具，还有很多其他功能，其中，最值得一提的是支付功能。

在中国，很多地方都支持手机支付，比如商场、饭店、公交车、地铁站，甚至在街边的小摊上买个煎饼都可以直接用手机来付钱。以前，交话费、水电费得去营业厅排队，给别人转账要去银行办理。现在这些事情，只要我们坐在家里动动手指，在手机上就可以完成，十分方便。

刚开始的时候，很多人不习惯用手机支付，担心手机支付不安全。但是，随着技术的提高，越来越多的人对手机支付已经很放心了。现在，你需要知道的是，如果手机没电了或者丢了该怎么办。

语言知识 Language guidelines

知识1 Tip 1

"从"

"我从没用过手机付钱"

副词"从"的意思和"从来"相同，表示过去到现在都是这样，多用于否定句。用否定词"没""没有"进行否定时，后面常加"过"。例如：

The adverb "从" means the same as "从来". It means the situation remains unchanged at all times up to now. It is often used in negative sentences. When negating with the negative word "没" or "没有", the sentence is often followed by "过". E. g. ,

(1) 我从不抽烟。

(2) 那个地方我从没去过。

(3) 这件事我从没有想过。

注意：在"从＋没/没有＋形容词"格式中，形容词前加"这么""这样"等词语后，句子的意思完全改变，甚至相反，因为"没""没有"否定的是"这么""这样"，而不是后面的形容词。例如：

Note: in the structure "从＋没/没有＋adjective", when words like "这么" and "这样" precede the adjective, the meaning of the sentence is completely changed, or even reversed, because "没" or "没有" negates "这么" or "这样", instead of the adjectives that follow. E. g. ,

（1）我从没紧张过。（以前到现在都不紧张，一直很放松。）

我从没这么紧张过。（以前也会紧张，但这一次最紧张。）

（2）他从没有开心过。（以前到现在都不开心。）

他从没有这样开心过。（以前也会开心，但这一次最开心。）

知识2 Tip 2

“弄”

“可我从没用过手机付钱，要怎么弄？”

1. 动词“弄”有“做”的意思，口语中常用。后面可以加“了”“着”“过”，可以重叠，还可以带名词性的宾语，所带宾语不同，“弄”的意义也会发生变化。例如：

The verb “弄” means “to do”, often used in spoken Chinese. It can be followed by “了”, “着” or “过”, and it can be used in reduplicated form. “弄” can take nominal objects, and its meaning varies depending on the object used. E. g. ,

（1）妈妈正在厨房弄着饭呢。（弄：做）

（2）我的电脑坏了，你帮我弄一下。（弄：修）

（3）这个语法，我还没弄懂。（弄：学习）

（4）今天有空儿，我要弄弄我的房间。（弄：打扫，整理）

（5）他把我的手机弄坏了。（弄：玩、摔等动作）

2. “弄”还有“想办法得到”的意思。后面常带数量词，还可以带“了”“过”。例如：

“弄” also means “to try to get”. In addition to “了” and “过”, it is often followed by a numeral-classifier compound. E. g. ,

（1）我弄来了一辆新车。

（2）我渴死了，帮我弄点儿水来。

（3）你能帮我们弄几张晚会的门票吗？

3. “弄+得……”多用在不好的方面。例如：

“弄+得……” is usually used in a disapproving way. E. g. ,

（1）你看，你把衣服弄得这么脏。

（2）他的话弄得大家都不开心。

（3）你弄得我也没办法了。

用法对比：“弄”和“搞”

Compare:“弄”and“搞”

1. 动词“弄”和“搞”都是随着搭配不同的宾语而有不同的意义。“弄”多用于口语，而“搞”既用于书面语，也用于口语。可以说“搞……工作”，不可以说“弄……工作”。例如：

The verbs “弄” and “搞” have different meanings due to different objects followed. “弄” is more commonly used in spoken Chinese; “搞” can be used both written and spoken language. The phrase “搞……工作” is acceptable, while “弄……工作” is not. E. g. ,

（1）我是搞翻译工作的。（*弄）

（2）你在公司搞什么工作？（*弄）

2. “弄”还有“玩弄，摆弄”的意思，可以重叠使用。例如：

“弄” also means “to play with”, and can be used in the reduplicated form. E. g.,

（1）你去别的地方玩，别弄那个花瓶！

（2）我平时喜欢弄弄花弄弄草，很少出去购物。

知识❸ Tip 3

“其他”

“还有很多其他功能”

代词“其他”的意思和“别的”相同，用于指代一定范围以外的人或事物。修饰单音节名词常加“的”，修饰双音节名词常常不需要加“的”，修饰代词“一切”时不带“的”。例如：

The pronoun “其他” has the same meaning as “别的” and is used to refer to people or things beyond a certain range. When it is used to modify monosyllabic nouns, the word “的” is often added; when it is used to modify disyllabic nouns, the word “的” is often omitted; when it is used to modify the pronoun “一切”, the word “的” is not used. E. g.,

（1）除了我以外，其他的人都去了。

除了我以外，其他（的）同学都去了。

（2）先看综合课的书，再看其他的书。

先写综合课的作业，再写其他（的）作业。

（3）这件事做好了，其他一切都不难了。

用法对比：“其他”和“别的”

Compare：“其他” and “别的”

1. “其他”和“别的”都可以用在名词前。“其他”后面可以加“的”，也可以不加。作宾语时，“其他”后面一般要加“的”，“别的”后面不加“的”。例如：

Both “其他” and “别的” can be used in front of nouns, and “的” following “其他” optional; when being part of the object, “其他” is generally followed by “的”, while “别的” should stand alone. E. g. ,

（1）除了我以外，其他（的）人都去了。

　　除了我以外，别的人都去了。

（2）饭还没做好，你先吃一些其他的。

　　饭还没做好，你先吃一些别的。

2. “其他”后面可以加数量词，“别的”不能。例如：

A numeral-classifier compound can be added after “其他”, but not for “别的”. E. g. ,

（1）我们坐公交回学校，其他四个人打的。（＊别的）

（2）其他几盘菜还没上，他就走了。（＊别的）

（3）只能坐这儿了，其他几排的票都没了。（＊别的）

知识4 Tip 4

“甚至”

“甚至在街边的小摊上买个煎饼都可以直接用手机来付钱”

1. 连词“甚至”放在并列的名词、形容词、动词、介词短语、小句的最后一项之前，强调突出的事例，有更进一层的意思，后面常有“都”“也”。例如：

The conjunction “甚至” is placed before the last one of a series of nouns, adjectives, verbs, prepositional phrases, or clauses. It is used for emphasis, implying higher intensity, often followed by “都” or “也”. E. g.,

(1) 今天的晚会很重要，同学、老师，甚至校长都来了。

(2) 弟弟的房间很乱，床上、桌上，甚至地上都是脏衣服。

(3) 她特别喜欢中文，上课下课都说中文，甚至睡觉时还在说中文。

(4) 这个箱子很重，甚至三个人也搬不动。

2. “甚至”一般用在后一小句，前一小句也常加“不但”。例如：

Usually, “甚至” is used in the latter clause, before which “不但” is often added. E. g.,

(1) 这个秘密，他不但没告诉朋友，甚至也没告诉他的妻子。

(2) 为了和她在一起，他不但搬了家，甚至换了一份新工作。

(3) 现在，不但年轻人喜欢玩手机，甚至老人也离不开手机。

3. “甚至”有时可以放在主语前。例如：

Sometimes “甚至” comes before the subject. E. g.,

（1）这个汉字很难，甚至老师也不知道怎么写。

（2）下周考试，甚至从不去图书馆的他也去图书馆看书了。

（3）他长得和中国人差不多，中文也好，甚至有人说他是中国人。

知识5 Tip 5

“随着”

“随着技术的提高，越来越多的人对手机支付已经很放心了。”

1. 介词“随着”常与名词和表示变化的双音节动词构成“随着＋名词＋的＋双音节动词”的结构，放在句首，也可以放在句中，表示一种情况的变化引起了另一种情况的出现或变化。例如：

The structure “随着 + noun + 的 + disyllabic verb”, in which the disyllabic verb indicat changes, is placed at the beginning of or in the middle of a sentence to indicate that the change of one situation causes the emergence or alteration of another one. E. g. ,

（1）随着社会的进步，人们的生活越来越好。

（2）随着春天的到来，天气越来越暖和。

（3）他随着中文水平的提高变得更自信了。

（4）我对这件事情的看法随着年纪的增长慢慢改变了。

2. “随着”还有动词的用法，即动词“随”加“着”，和介词“随着”一样，也有“跟着，跟随”的意思。例如：

Divided into the verb “随” and the particle “着”, “随着” can also function as a verb, referring to “to follow” as its prepositional counterpart. E. g. ,

（1）孩子哭了，妈妈也随着哭了。

（2）看到班长站起来，大家也随着他一起站起来。

（3）听到别的班的同学唱生日歌，我的心也随着歌声飞走了。

练习 Exercises

1. **词语搭配**。Complete the phrases.

________支付	绑定________	打开________
设置________	________二维码	其他________
________功能	成为________	担心________
交________	________提高	________密码

2. **选词填空**。Choose the right words to fill in the blanks.

完成　随着　值得　设置　绑定　甚至　支付　成为

（1）在中国，很多商店都可以用手机________。

（2）儿子，你长大了想________什么样的人？

（3）这么多作业，你今天能________吗？

（4）________中国的快速发展，越来越多的外国人来中国学习中文。

（5）想用手机支付先要________支付密码。

（6）我觉得花 1000 块钱买一双鞋子不________。

（7）我特别喜欢喝奶茶，每天都会喝，________睡觉都想着它。

（8）我的微信没有________银行卡，所以不能使用微信支付。

3. 选词填空。Choose the right words to fill in the blanks.

其他　　别的

（1）我只买了综合课的书，__________的书还没买。

（2）这个办法我试过了，没有用，还有__________办法吗？

（3）这个颜色不好，请帮我换个__________。

（4）除了白云山，你还知道__________好玩儿的地方吗？

（5）这边的东西都不打折，我们去看看__________的。

（6）老师说只做这一题，__________两题不用做。

4. 改错句。Correct the sentences.

（1）我从没有见过中国的长城了。

____

（2）随着中文水平的提高，越来越喜欢中国的文化。

____

（3）今天不忙，我要弄洗衣服。

____

（4）他十分很有钱。

____

（5）你在学校弄什么工作？

____

（6）茶有很多种，红茶是其中茶。

____

（7）飞机里有三百多人，其中我的朋友。

____

5. 组句。 Rearrange the words to form a sentence.

(1) 加号　在　首页　的　右上角　有　微信　一个

____

(2) 密码　设置　付款　先要　你

____

(3) 伙伴　人们　生活中　手机　重要　成为　的　已经

____

(4) 功能　的　最　值得一提　支付　是

____

(5) 生活　技术　提高　越来越　随着　的　方便

____

(6) 担心　问题　支付　手机　安全　人们　的

____

6. 完成句子。 Complete the sentences.

(1) ________________，这是我第一次用，你能帮我吗？（从没）

(2) 中国有很多有名的大城市，________________。（比如）

(3) 中国文化很有意思，________________。（其中）

(4) 手机有很多功能，________________。（值得一提）

(5) 这是秘密，________________。（其他）

(6) 他很忙，________________。（甚至）

(7) 广州，________________。（不仅……还……）

(8) ________________，出国旅游越来越方便。（随着）

7. 根据课文回答问题。Answer the questions according to the text.

课文 1

（1）买东西的时候，阿里有什么麻烦？该怎么办？

____

（2）怎么用手机付钱？

____

课文 2

（1）刚开始的时候，很多人觉得手机支付怎么样？为什么？

____

（2）现在人们的想法有什么变化？

____

（3）手机支付可以帮人们做什么？

____

（4）除了支付功能，手机还有哪些其他功能？

____

（5）对你来说，手机的哪一种功能最值得一提？

____

8. 我是微信专家。I am the expert of WeChat.

（1）比一比微信和支付宝的支付功能，说一说它们有什么相同和不同。

支付手段	相同	不同
微信		
支付宝		

（2）比一比微信和其他的社交软件，比如 QQ、Facebook、Line 等，说一说它们有什么相同和不同。

社交软件	相同	不同
微信		

（3）你希望给微信加上哪些新的功能？问一问你的朋友，拍一个小视频。

9. **小练笔**。Writing.

没有手机的一天（不少于100个字）

我的手机坏了，早上刚拿去修，师傅说明天才能修好，所以今天我……

第二课　出门靠朋友

Rely on friends when you go out

课前热身 Warming up

你觉得朋友重要吗？你有中国朋友吗？

Do you think friends are important? Do you have Chinese friends?

生词 New words

1	课间	kèjiān	名	break (between classes)
2	哟*	yō	叹	used to express a slight surprise (sometimes in a joking tone)

3	摔	shuāi	动	to fall; to lose one's balance; to cause to fall and break
4	伤	shāng	名/动	wound; injury; to injure; to hurt
5	受伤	shòushāng	动	to be injured; to be wounded
6	医务室	yīwù shì		infirmary; clinic
7	楼梯	lóutī	名	stairs
8	暗	àn	形	dark; dim; dull
9	不小心	bù xiǎo xīn		to be careless; to take care; careful
	小心	xiǎo xīn	动/形	to be careful; to take care; careful
10	照顾	zhàogù	动	to look after; to care for; to give consideration to; to take account of
11	靠	kào	动	to lean; to lean against; to depend on; to rely on; to get close to; to be near to
12	帮助	bāngzhù	动	to help
13	困难	kùnnan	形/名	difficult; hard; difficulty; trouble
14	一……就……	yī……jiù……		as soon as
15	亲爱	qīn'ài	形	dear; beloved

16	一切	yíqiè	代	all; every; everything
17	顺利	shùnlì	形	smooth; successful
18	说实话	shuō shíhuà		to tell the truth; to be honest
	实话	shíhuà	名	truth
19	遇到	yù dào		to encounter; to come across
20	恨不得	hènbude	动	to be very anxious to; to wish one could
21	回国	huí guó		to return home from abroad
22	幸运	xìngyùn	名/形	good fortune; good luck; fortunate; lucky
23	班主任	bānzhǔrèn	名	a teacher in charge of a class; class teacher
24	关心	guānxīn	动	to be concerned with; to care for
25	互相	hùxiāng	副	mutually
26	适应	shìyìng	动	to adapt to
27	健康	jiànkāng	形	healthy

课文 Text

课文 1 Text 1

（课间，阿里、米亚、艾文三人在聊天。）

艾文：哟，班长今天没来上课，真是"太阳从西边出来了"。

阿里：别开玩笑了！听说班长昨天晚上摔伤了，去了医院。

米亚：是的，她现在还在医院呢。

艾文：你是怎么知道的？

米亚：昨天晚上她打电话给我，说她受伤了。我先带她去了医务室，医务室的医生说得去医院，所以我又陪她去了医院。

阿里：这么严重？怎么搞的？

米亚：她说昨晚爬楼梯的时候，灯太暗了，不小心摔下来了。

阿里：那现在谁在医院照顾她？

米亚：她的中国朋友早上去医院了。

艾文：一个人在国外，朋友真的很重要啊。

米亚：是的，在家靠父母，出门靠朋友。平时班长总是帮助大家，现在她有困难了，我们应该帮助她。

艾文：说得对！我们找个时间一起去医院看看她吧。

阿里：好啊，我们一下课就去。

课文2 Text 2

亲爱的爸爸、妈妈：

你们好！

身体怎么样？一切都顺利吗？我在中国很好，你们不用担心。

说实话，刚来中国的时候，我一点儿也不习惯，中文不好，又没有朋友。每次遇到困难，我都恨不得马上回国。

但幸运的是，我们的班主任很好，不仅关心我们的学习，也关心我们的生活。同学们也互相关心、互相帮助。上次我摔伤了，班里的一位同学送我去了医院，其他同学下课后还去医院看我呢。靠同学朋友的帮助，我很快就适应了这里的生活。现在，我每天都过得很开心。

对了，你们一定会问我学习怎么样？完全不用担心，我的中文说得流利着呢！

先写到这里吧。祝爸妈身体健康！

安娜

2023 年 9 月 20 日

语言知识 Language guidelines

知识 1 Tip 1

“靠”

“在家靠父母，出门靠朋友。”

“靠同学朋友的帮助，我很快就适应了这里的生活。”

动词“靠”有“在……的帮助下”“依靠……”的意思。例如：

The verb “靠” means “with the help of ...” and “depending on...”. E. g. ,

(1) 靠自己的努力，我考了 100 分。

(2) 他靠手机上的地图 App，找到了那家饭店。

(3) 爷爷的眼睛不好，看报纸上的小字得靠眼镜。

(4) A：你的朋友真多！

B：是啊，在家靠父母，出门靠朋友。朋友多了不想家。

知识❷ Tip 2

"一……就……" 教学视频

"我们一下课就去"

"一……就……"表示两个动作或情况紧接着发生。例如：

"一……就……" indicates that two actions or situations happen next to each other. E. g. ,

(1) 我一回家就给他打电话。

(2) 老师一说，我就明白了。

(3) 我真幸运，一到家，就开始下雨了。

"一……就……"还表示一到某种条件就会出现某种情况。例如：

"一……就……" also means that once a certain condition is met, something will happen. E. g. ,

(1) 我已经买了飞机票，一放假就回国。

(2) 我晚上不喝咖啡，因为我一喝咖啡就睡不着。

(3) 他是我最好的朋友，我一遇到困难，他就会帮助我。

知识❸ Tip 3

"一切"

"一切都顺利吗？"

代词"一切"表示"全部、各种"，常和"都"一起使用。作定语时不加"的"。例如：

The pronoun “一切” means “all, every”, often used together with “都”. It should not be followed by “的” when used as an attributive. E. g.,

(1) 我一切都很好。
(2) 这儿的一切都很有意思。
(3) 来中国的一切事情都是我自己做的。
(4) 这次事故让他失去了一切。

用法对比：“一切”和“所有”

Compare: “一切” and “所有”

“一切”和“所有”都有“全部包括，没有例外的”的意思。“所有”指一定范围内（如一定时间、空间，某人或某些人）所领有的、所存在的全部数量。“所有”可以形容各种人和事物（不管可不可以分类），和定语之间常加“的”，也可以不加。例如：

Both “一切” and “所有” mean “all-inclusive without exception”. “所有” means the total amount possessed or existing within a certain range (e. g., a certain time, space, individual or group). “所有” can be used to describe all kinds of people and things (whether they can be classified or not), and “的” is dispensable between it and the attributive. E. g.,

(1) 家里所有（的）房间妈妈都打扫了一遍。
(2) 做完了所有（的）工作，他才去休息。
(3) 我们把所有的钱都花完了。

“一切”指代所包含的全部类别，只修饰可以分类的人和事物，和定语之间常不加“的”。例如：

“一切” refers to all the categories contained, and only modifies the people and things that can be classified, and “的” is always omitted between it and attributive. E. g. ,

（1）我喜欢这个地方，它的一切我都感兴趣。

（2）这里的一切工作都十分顺利。

（3）一切困难都会有办法的。

知识4 Tip 4

“恨不得”

“每次遇到困难，我都恨不得马上回国。”

动词“恨不得”表示急切希望做成某事（多用于实际做不到的事情），后面一定要带动词作宾语。“恨不得”和动词宾语之间常用“马上”“立刻”“赶快”“都”“就”“全”等副词或带“一”的动量词。例如：

The verb “恨不得” is used to express the fervent wish that something (usually something impossible) can be done. It should always take a verbal object, and adverbs “马上” “立刻” “赶快” “都” “就” “全” or action-measure complements with “一” are often added between. E. g. ,

（1）听说妈妈病了，我恨不得马上飞回去看她。

（2）这些衣服又便宜又漂亮，她恨不得全买了。

（3）考试前，我恨不得一下子记住所有的词语。

(4) 他太饿了，恨不得一口吃完一碗米饭。

练习 Exercises

1. 词语搭配。 Complete the phrases.

照顾________	帮助________	一切________
遇到________	关心________	适应________
________困难	________实话	________顺利

2. 选词填空。 Choose the right words to fill in the blanks.

恨不得	受伤	幸运	帮助	回国
靠	互相	摔	适应	顺利

(1) 你真________，这是今天最后一班公交车。

(2) 我刚来中国，还不________这里的生活。

(3) 如果一切________，这项工作两天就能做好。

(4) 他总是________大家，我们都很喜欢他。

(5) 我的中文好，他的英文好，平时我们________学习。

(6) 听到妈妈生病的消息，我________马上回国。

(7) 刚学骑车的时候，我常常从自行车上________下来。

(8) 在一次比赛中，我的腿________了。

(9) 毕业以后，我想________工作。

(10) 他________自己工作挣的钱读完了大学。

3. **改错句**。Correct the sentences.

(1) 我们应该关心对自己的分数。

____

(2) 这本书不仅很难也很有意思。

____

(3) 最近太累了，我恨不得不想工作。

____

(4) 刚来的时候，我一点儿适应这里的生活。

____

(5) 昨天晚上我摔倒了，受伤了我的手。

____

(6) 亲爱爸爸妈妈，你们身体怎么样？

____

(7) 他们一切的事情都很顺利。

____

(8) 我买了一本中文书，还要买其他本书。

____

4. **组句**。Rearrange the words to form a sentence.

(1) 摔伤　昨天　了　班长　晚上　听说

____

(2) 大家　平时　学习　他　中文　帮助

____

(3) 同学　医院　来看　下课后　其他　我

____

（4）流利　中文　说得　我的　着呢

____

（5）遇到　一　困难　恨不得　我就　回国　马上

____

5. **完成句子**。Complete the sentences.

（1）A：你的中文为什么这么好？

B：______________________。（靠）

（2）A：你觉得中国的生活怎么样？

B：______________________。（说实话）

（3）我朋友特别爱玩手机，______________________。（恨不得）

（4）老师，今天我有重要的事，我得______________________

______________________。（一……就……）

（5）刚来中国的时候，______________________。（一切）

（6）A：什么是好朋友？

B：______________________。（互相）

（7）A：你怎么在医务室？

B：朋友病了，我来照顾他，______________________？（对了）

（8）他去晚了，______________________。（幸运）

6. **根据课文回答问题**。Answer the questions according to the text.

课文 1

（1）"太阳从西边出来了"是什么意思？艾文为什么这么说？

____

（2）班长是怎么受伤的？为什么会受伤？

___

（3）同学们打算下课后做什么？为什么？

___

课文 2

（1）安娜刚来中国的时候怎么样？为什么？

___

（2）现在有什么变化？为什么会有这样的变化？

___

7. **朋友小调查**。Finish a survey about friends.

（1）说一说你最喜欢或者最讨厌朋友的哪些方面，为什么？

	为什么
最喜欢	
最讨厌	

（2）你什么时候会帮助朋友？什么时候不会帮助他？为什么？

___

___

___

8. 小练笔。Writing.

给家人写一封信，介绍你在中国的学习和生活，可以加上你的照片，注意信的格式。（不少于 100 个字）

亲爱的__________：

____

____

____

____

____

____

____

____

____

____

____年____月____日

第三课　我的脚扭伤了

I sprained my foot

课前热身 Warming up

运动的时候，如果不小心伤到了，你会怎么办？

What would you do if you hurt yourself while exercising?

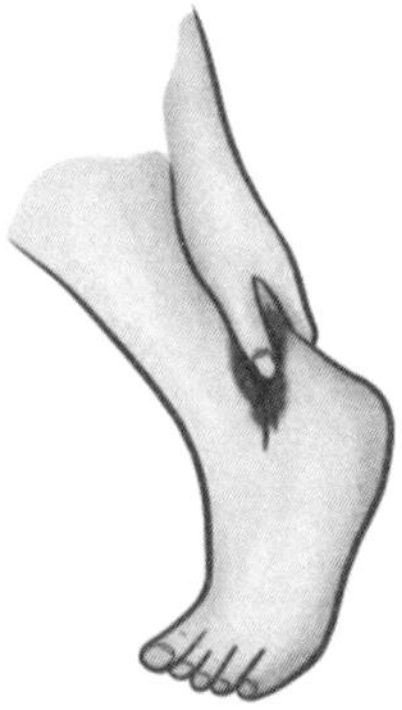

生词 New words

1	扭	niǔ	动	to sprain；to wrench；to twist；to rurn round
2	卷	juǎn	动	to roll up
3	裤脚	kùjiǎo	名	bottom of a trouser leg

4	脚踝	jiǎo huái		ankle
5	肿	zhǒng	动	to swell
6	踢	tī	动	to kick; to play
7	结果	jiéguǒ	名/连	result; out come; finally; at last
8	走路	zǒulù	动	to walk
9	骨折	gǔzhé	动	(of a bone) to break; to suffer a fracture
10	拍	pāi	动	to clap; to pat; to beat; to take (a picture); to shoot
11	片子	piānzi	名	X-ray image; film; gramophone record
12	骨头	gǔtou	名	bone
13	病历	bìnglì	名	medical record
14	消肿	xiāozhǒng	动	to reduce swelling
15	走动	zǒudòng	动	to walk out; to move around
16	药房	yàofáng	名	drugstore; hospital pharmacy
17	倒霉	dǎoméi	形	have bad luck; be out of luck
18	正常	zhèngcháng	形	normal; regular
19	扶	fú	动	to support with the hand; to help sb. up
20	墙	qiáng	名	wall

21	慢	màn	形	slow
22	挪	nuó	动	to move; to shift
23	蜗牛*	wōniú	名	snail
24	药店	yàodiàn	名	drugstore; pharmacy
25	膏药*	gāoyao	名	medicated plaster
26	贴	tiē	动	to stick; to paste
27	检查	jiǎnchá	动	to check up; to inspect
28	问题	wèntí	名	question; problem
29	口服药	kǒufú yào		oral medicine
	口服	kǒufú	动	to take orally
30	喷雾*	pēn wù		mist spray
31	服药	fúyào	动	to take medicine
32	毛巾	máojīn	名	towel
33	敷*	fū	动	to apply (powder, medical ointement, etc)

课文 Text

课文 1 Text 1

医生：你怎么了？

林一：医生，我的脚扭伤了。都好几天了，还是疼得厉害。

医生：在哪里？我看看……

林一：（卷起裤脚）在这儿，脚踝这里。

医生：呀，肿得挺厉害的，怎么扭伤的？

林一：踢足球的时候不小心扭到了。

医生：伤了几天了？

林一：三四天了，原来想着休息休息就没事儿了，结果这两天走路疼得厉害，是骨折了吗？

医生：你最好先去拍张片子，然后拿片子过来找我。

…………

林一：医生，怎么样？很严重吗？

医生：还好，没伤到骨头。你的病历给我，我给你开点消肿的药，最近半个月不要走动太多，交费后，去一楼药房拿药。

林一：好的，谢谢医生。

课文❷ Text 2

我的朋友林一最近特别倒霉，先是钱包丢了，然后是写完的作业找不到了，上个星期我们踢足球的时候，他的脚踝又扭伤了，结果不能正常走路，只能扶着墙慢慢地挪，像一只蜗牛一样。扭伤的第一天，我帮他去药店买了一些膏药，让他贴在扭伤的地方。但是他休息了没两天，脚踝肿得更厉害了，我只好陪他去医院检查。

不过幸运的是，医生检查了以后说没有什么大问题，给他开了两种药，一种是口服药，另一种是喷雾。医生告诉他，口服药一天三次，饭后吃，每天要按时服药；用喷雾之前，先用热毛巾敷一下扭伤的地方。这段时间，一定不要经常走动，要多休息，两个星期以后应该就没事儿了。

语言知识 Language guidelines

知识 1 Tip 1

"都……了" 教学视频

"都好几天了"

副词"都"表示"已经"的意思，通常和"了"组成"都……了"，中间多加数量词、时间词或某些名词，表示"数量多""年龄大""时间晚"等。例如：

The adverb "都" refe to "already", often followed by "了" to form "都……了". Numeral-classifier compounds, temporal words or some nouns are often added in the middle of the structure to indicate large amount, old age, lateness of the hour and so on. E. g. ,

（1）饭都凉了，快点儿吃吧。

（2）这个字我都写了三十遍了，还是记不住。

（3）你都是大人了，怎么还看动画片？

（4）都中午了，他还在睡觉。

知识 2 Tip 2

"……得厉害"

"疼得厉害""肿得挺厉害的"

"……得厉害"用来表示病情、问题等的程度很深，常指让人感到不舒服、麻烦。例如：

"……得厉害" is used to indicate a high degree of illnesses, troubles, etc. , implying the discomfort and inconvenience brought by the mentioned problems. E. g. ,

(1) 我感冒了，头疼得厉害。

(2) 医生说他要住院一个星期，没想到他病得这么厉害。

(3) 今天星期一，路上堵车堵得厉害。

(4) 最近没复习，中文退步得很厉害。

知识3 Tip 3

“结果”

“结果这两天走路疼得厉害”“结果不能正常走路”

连词“结果”表示在某种条件或情况下产生某种结局，常用在后一小句。例如：

The conjunction “结果” indicates a certain outcome under certain conditions or circumstances, often used in the latter clause. E. g. ,

(1) 我太紧张了，结果忘记写名字了。

(2) 我们坐错了公交车，结果来到了一个不认识的地方。

(3) 他们比过一次赛，结果成了好朋友。

知识4 Tip 4

“还”

“还好，没伤到骨头。”

副词“还”有一种用法是“还+形容词”，表示在程度上勉强过得去，基本上达到要求。其中的形容词多是褒义，常用下降语气表达。例如：

“还 + adjective” indicates that something is barely acceptable and basically meets the requirements. Mostly positive the adjectives in this structure get toned down or weakened by “还”. E. g. ,

（1）A：最近身体怎么样？

B：还好/还行/还可以。

（2）我的汉字写得不好，口语发音还不错。

（3）我的家虽然不大，但还干净，欢迎你来做客。

（4）那件衣服一千块，这件八百块，两件相比，这件还比较便宜。

练习 Exercises

1. 词语搭配。Complete the phrases.

拍________	踢________	挪________
________问题	贴________	检查________
敷________	骨头________	按时________

2. 选词填空。Choose the right words to fill in the blanks.

正常　结果　倒霉　按时　还　片子　走动　厉害

（1）刚一出门，就开始下雨，真________。

（2）爷爷现在腿脚不好，所以不经常去外面________了。

（3）医生让你________吃药，你总是不听，现在病得更厉害了。

（4）医生看了刚拍的＿＿＿＿＿，告诉我，我的病不严重。

（5）我的电脑总是自己关机，有点不＿＿＿＿＿。

（6）老师说我这次考得＿＿＿＿＿不错，我自己也比较满意。

（7）我头疼得＿＿＿＿＿，我得到床上休息一下。

（8）我起床起晚了，＿＿＿＿＿迟到了。

3. 按要求完成句子。Complete the sentences as required.

A. 用“还”完成句子。

（1）他的汉字写得＿＿＿＿＿＿＿＿＿＿＿＿＿＿＿＿。

（2）医生说我的身体＿＿＿＿＿＿＿＿＿＿＿＿，没有太大问题。

（3）上周末我去了一次香港，我觉得香港＿＿＿＿＿＿＿＿＿＿。

（4）这件衣服好看，价格＿＿＿＿＿＿＿＿＿＿＿，就买这件吧。

（5）11 点多食堂排队的人＿＿＿＿一点儿，12 点下课后人太多了。

（6）这家店我吃过几次，味道＿＿＿＿＿＿＿＿＿＿＿＿＿＿＿。

B. 用“都……了”改写句子。

（1）现在晚上 12 点了，你怎么还在玩手机？

＿＿＿＿＿＿＿＿＿＿＿＿＿＿＿＿＿＿＿＿＿＿＿＿＿＿＿＿＿＿

（2）他已经 40 岁了，还没有结婚。

＿＿＿＿＿＿＿＿＿＿＿＿＿＿＿＿＿＿＿＿＿＿＿＿＿＿＿＿＿＿

（3）你已经是大学生了，还喜欢小孩子的玩具吗？

＿＿＿＿＿＿＿＿＿＿＿＿＿＿＿＿＿＿＿＿＿＿＿＿＿＿＿＿＿＿

（4）我们等了 2 个小时了，他为什么还没有来？

＿＿＿＿＿＿＿＿＿＿＿＿＿＿＿＿＿＿＿＿＿＿＿＿＿＿＿＿＿＿

（5）你吃了 3 碗面条了，还没有吃饱吗？

＿＿＿＿＿＿＿＿＿＿＿＿＿＿＿＿＿＿＿＿＿＿＿＿＿＿＿＿＿＿

C. 看图片用“……得厉害”写句子。

(1) ______________

(2) ______________

(3) ______________

(4) ______________

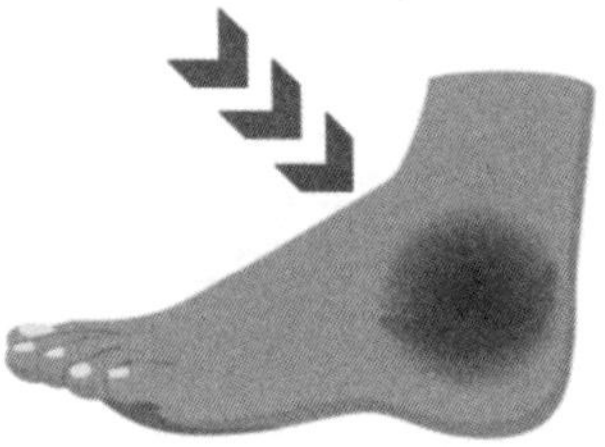

(5) ______________

(6) ______________

4. 改错句。 Correct the sentences.

(1) 我喜欢拍照漂亮的风景。

____

（2）以前买过的裤子的裤脚现在有点儿短。

____

（3）孩子三岁的时候可以走动了。

____

（4）我的脚扭伤了，结果老板让我家里休息两天再上班。

____

（5）我喜欢喝牛奶，结果我的骨头很强壮。

____

5. 完成句子。 Complete the sentences.

（1）我今天出门没带伞，______________________。（结果）

（2）昨天我吃了不新鲜的菜，__________________。（结果）

（3）我的作业不见了，______________________。（结果）

（4）明天考试，大家要______________________。（按时）

（5）他______________________，需要住院。（严重）

（6）我吃了药以后，______________________。（正常）

（7）考试时______________________。（检查）

（8）下课的时候，同学们____________________。（问题）

6. 根据课文回答问题。 Answer the questions according to the text.

课文 1

（1）林一去了哪儿？他怎么了？

____

（2）他的伤严重吗？你怎么知道的？

____

课文 2

（1）林一最近怎么样？

____

（2）“我”为什么陪他去医院？

____

（3）林一要住院吗？为什么？

____

（4）医生给林一看病的时候说了哪些话？

____

7．**看病知多少**。Do you know how to go to the doctor?

（1）你知道怎么看病吗？下面的词语你都知道吗？

guàhào 挂号 register at hospital	nèikē 内科 internal medicine	wàikē 外科 surgical department

 bìnglì 病历 medical record	 jiǎnchá 检查 examination	 huàyàn 化验 laboratory test
 jiāo fèi 交 费 pay the fee	 yàofáng 药房 hospital pharmacy	 ná yào 拿 药 get the medicine

（2）用上面的词语完成对话。

（在医院）

病人：护士，我要__________。

护士：你要挂什么科？

病人：__________。

护士：你带__________吗？

病人：带了，谢谢。

…………

医生：你哪里不舒服？

病人：我最近拉肚子拉得厉害，不知道什么原因，您能帮我＿＿＿＿＿一下吗？

医生：我给你开化验单，你先去＿＿＿＿＿吧，拿到化验结果以后再过来找我。

病人：好的。

…………

病人：医生，我的病严重吗？

医生：没有太大问题，我给你开一些药，你先去＿＿＿＿＿，然后去＿＿＿＿＿拿药吧。

8．小练笔。Writing.

我生病了（不少于 100 个字）

昨天我和朋友出去玩，＿＿＿＿＿＿＿＿＿＿＿＿＿＿＿＿＿＿＿＿

第四课　租房

Rent a house

课前热身 Warming up

你住在学校宿舍还是在外面租房？你知道在中国怎么租房吗？

Do you live in the school dormitory or rent an apartment outside the campus? Do you know how to rent an apartment in China?

生词 New words

1	合租	hézū	动	to rent jointly
	租	zū	动	to hire; to rent; to rent out; to let out
2	套	tào	量/名/动	set; suit; cover; case; to cover with

3	算	suàn	动	to calculate; to count; to consider as; to regard as
4	平方米	píngfāngmǐ	量	square meter
	平方	píngfāng	名/量	square; square meter
5	卧室*	wòshì	名	bedroom
6	客厅	kètīng	名	living room
7	厨房*	chúfáng	名	kitchen
8	房屋	fángwū	名	house; buildings
9	中介	zhōngjiè	名	intermediary agent
10	吵	chǎo	形/动	noisy; to disturb by making noise; to quarrel
11	挑剔	tiāoti	动	to nitpick; to be hypercritical
12	可	kě	连/副	but; yet; (used for emphasis)
13	谨慎	jǐnshèn	形	prudent; carful; cautious
14	贵客	guìkè	名	honoured guest
15	随时	suíshí	副	at any time; when ever necessary
16	应	yìng	动	to answer; to respond to; to accept (an invitation)
17	邀请	yāoqǐng	动	to invite

18	公寓	gōngyù	名	flats; apartment house; lodging house
19	周围	zhōuwéi	名	around; surrounding
20	正门	zhèngmén	名	front door; gate; main entrance
21	便利	biànlì	形	convenient
22	稍微	shāowēi	副	a little; a bit; slightly
23	睡懒觉	shuì lǎnjiào		get up late; sleep in; sleep late
24	阳台	yángtái	名	balcony
25	宽敞	kuānchang	形	spacious; commodious; roomy
26	空气	kōngqì	名	air
27	流通	liútōng	动	to circulate
28	阳光	yángguāng	名	sunlight; sunshine
29	隐私	yǐnsī	名	privacy
30	房东	fángdōng	名	landlord
31	安装	ānzhuāng	动	to install; to mount
32	地段	dìduàn	名	a section of an area
33	租金	zūjīn	名	rental
34	更不用说	gèng búyòng shuō		not to mention; not to speak of
35	网费	wǎng fèi		Internet bill
36	物业管理费	wùyè guǎnlǐ fèi		property management fee

物业	wùyè	名	property；real estate
管理	guǎnlǐ	动	to manage；to administer

课文 Text

课文1 Text 1

阿里：你住学校宿舍吗？

艾文：不，我和朋友在外面合租了一套房子。

阿里：哇！在哪儿？

艾文：在北京路附近，坐地铁很方便，不过离学校有点儿远。

阿里：房子大不大？

艾文：不算大，五六十平方米，有两个卧室和一个客厅，还有一个大厨房。

阿里：听起来挺不错的，你是什么时候租的？

艾文：开学前。我提前来到广州，跟朋友一起去了房屋中介，让中介帮我们找的。

阿里：找房子麻烦吗？

艾文：可麻烦啦！不是太贵、太小，就是交通不方便、太吵或者不太安全。

阿里：哈哈，你真挑剔！不过租房子可得谨慎，出门在外，安全第一。什么时候请我去参观参观？

艾文：你可是贵客，随时欢迎。

课文 2 Text 2

今天我应朋友的邀请，去他的新家做客。这个学期他没有住在宿舍，而是和朋友合租了一套公寓。在那里生活方便得很，小区周围有很多超市、银行，还有一座大商场和一家医院。没事的时候，还可以去附近的公园散散步。离小区正门不远，是一个地铁站，走路大概花五分钟就到了，交通十分便利。不过，公寓离学校稍微有点儿远，他为了不迟到，再也没睡过懒觉了。

这套公寓是两室一厅，客厅和阳台都挺宽敞的，空气流通，阳光很好，每个人都有自己的卧室，再也不用担心隐私问题了。房东还为他们安装了 Wi-Fi，上网可快了。不过，因为地段好，环境也不错，所以这套公寓的租金不便宜，一个月要三千多，更不用说每个月还要交水电费、网费、物业管理费了。这可比住宿舍贵多了，我还是住学校宿舍吧！

语言知识 Language guidelines

知识 1 Tip 1

“算”

“不算大，五六十平方米”

1. 动词“算”后面常加形容词、名词或者动词，意思是“认为是，可以说是”，用来表示对事物的判断。例如：

The verb “算” is often followed by an adjective, a noun, or a verb to make a judgment about something. E. g. ,

（1）你的手机2000块，不算贵。（算+形容词）

（2）他教过我几节课，算是我的老师。（算+名词）

（3）A：你认识他吗？

B：我和他吃过一次饭，算认识吧。（算+动词）

2. 通常，说话人是以人们的常识或普遍认同的标准作为判断的参照，常常不需要说出参照物。但作比较时，说话人会将判断所参照的标准或事物明确表达出来。例如：

Usually, the speaker takes common sense or generally accepted standard as the reference of judgment, and there is no need to point out the reference in the sentence. But in comparison, the speaker makes it clear what criteria or things the judgment is based on. E. g. ,

句中不说出参照物	句中说出参照物
这部手机五千块算贵的。	和老板的新手机比，这部五千块钱，不算贵。
你考了90分，算考得很好了。	在我们班，90分很多，不算考得很好的。
今天15度，不算暖和。	昨天10度，今天15度，还算暖和了。

知识❷ Tip 2

"不是……，就是……" 教学视频

"不是太贵、太小，就是交通不方便、太吵或者不太安全。"

1. "不是……，就是……"常表示两种情况当中必有其一。例如：

“不是……，就是……” indicates that there must be one of two conditions. E. g. ,

（1）下午的会议只能班长参加，所以不是正班长去就是副班长去。

（2）这道题只有两个选择，不是A对，就是B对。

（3）最近要考试，他不是在图书馆看书，就是在宿舍学习。

2. “不是……，就是……”也用来列举某一情况的各种表现。例如：

“不是……，就是……” is also used to illustrate various manifestations of a certain circumstance. E. g. ,

（1）他特别爱运动，下课后不是去操场跑步，就是去打篮球、踢足球。

（2）周末，我不是去公园散步，就是去逛超市，不常待在家里。

（3）我常常生病，不是拉肚子，就是感冒。

知识3 Tip 3

“可”

“可麻烦啦”“租房子可得谨慎”“你可是贵客”“上网可快了”

副词“可”表示强调语气，强调语气的程度由轻到重都有，多用于口语。

The adverb “可” is used to indicate emphasis, the intensity of which is reliant on the context. It is mostly used in spoken Chinese.

1. 用于一般陈述句，有时稍有出乎意料的意思，强调语气的程度最轻。例如：

When used in a general declarative sentence, it sometimes suggests that something is beyond the speaker's expectations, laying the slightest emphasis on the statement. E. g.,

（1）这句话我可没说过，你别乱说。

（2）我可知道他的性格，只要他说了就一定会去做。

（3）手机没电了，这可是一个大问题。

2. 用于祈使句。强调必须如此，有时有恳切劝导的意思。后面一般有“要”“能”“应该”，句末多有语气助词，强调语气的程度较重。例如：

When it is used in an imperative sentence, it means “something must get done”, sometimes implying sincere persuasion. Generally, it is followed by “要”, “能” and “应该”, with a modal particle standing at the end of the sentence. There is a heavy emphasis on the statement. E. g.,

（1）妈妈，我的毕业晚会，你可要来啊！

（2）这次考试很重要，你可不能迟到！

（3）明天8点在东门集合，你可别忘了啊！

3. 用于感叹句。句末用语气助词，强调语气的程度最重。例如：

When it is used in an exclamatory sentence, a mood particle should be used at the end of the sentence. The emphasis indicated by “可” in this case is the heaviest among the mentioned structures. E. g.,

(1) 他的篮球打得可好啦!

(2) 现在下午6点多，地铁上的人可多了，我们还是晚点去吧!

(3) 89路公交车可来了，我都等了15分钟了。

知识4 Tip 4

存现句

"小区周围有很多超市、银行。"

存现句表示某个地方存在、出现或者消失了某人或某物。

An existential sentence means that someone or something exists, appears, or disappears in a certain place.

存现句的基本句型:

The basic sentence structure:

处所词 + 动词 + 宾语
location word + verb + object

其中，句首的处所词可以是名词、方位词、代词等，谓语动词后的宾语通常由不确指的数量词加名词充当，名词前一般不能带有确指意义的定语。例如:

Among them, the location word at the beginning of a sentence can be a noun, a directional word, a pronoun, etc., and the object after the verbal predicate is usually served by an indefinite numeral-classifier compound followed by a noun. Generally, the attributives with definite meanings cannot be used before a noun. E. g. ,

(1) 桌子上有一本书和几支笔。

（2）我家小区前面是一个公园。

（3）停车场停着很多车。

（4）楼上走下来一位老奶奶。

（5）窗前刚飞走两只小鸟。

知识 5 Tip 5

“更不用说”

“一个月要三千多，更不用说每个月还要交水电费、网费、物业管理费了。”

“更不用说”表示的是一种递进关系，句子常写成“情况 A，更不用说 + 情况 B”，意思是相比于情况 A，情况 B 更有可能或更不可能。当情况 A 为肯定句时，情况 B 更有可能；当情况 A 为否定句时，情况 B 更不可能。例如：

“更不用说”, suggesting a progressive relationship, is often used in the structure “case A, 更不用说 + case B”, with the meaning that case B is more or less likely than case A. When the main clause is an affirmative one, case B is more likely than case A; otherwise, case B is even less likely than case A. E. g. ,

情况 A 为肯定句	情况 A 为否定句
这个字我们都认识，更不用说老师了。	这个字老师也不认识，更不用说我们了。
我能爬六楼，更不用说二楼了。	我二楼都爬不动，更不用说六楼了。

（续上表）

情况 A 为肯定句	情况 A 为否定句
他在广州十年，更不用说去过广州塔。	他没来过广州，更不用说去过广州塔了。

练习 Exercises

1．**词语搭配**。Complete the phrases.

租＿＿＿＿＿	邀请＿＿＿＿＿	＿＿＿＿＿周围
管理＿＿＿＿＿	＿＿＿＿＿流通	＿＿＿＿＿中介
随时＿＿＿＿＿	安装＿＿＿＿＿	＿＿＿＿＿隐私
租金＿＿＿＿＿	＿＿＿＿＿便利	地段＿＿＿＿＿

2．**选词填空**。Choose the right words to fill in the blanks.

周围　挑剔　谨慎　便利　稍微　阳光　套　吵　宽敞

（1）她买东西特别＿＿＿＿＿，选了半天也没选好。

（2）昨晚我没有睡好，因为旁边的房间太＿＿＿＿＿了。

（3）我的老板在广州最好的地段买了一＿＿＿＿＿房子。

（4）我家附近有地铁站也有公交站，出门特别＿＿＿＿＿。

（5）跟我现在的家相比，这间老房子不够＿＿＿＿＿。

（6）这件衣服太贵了，能不能＿＿＿＿＿便宜一点儿？

（7）外面的＿＿＿＿＿真好，我们去散散步吧！

（8）他是一个很＿＿＿＿＿的人，做事前都会想想怎么做，想好了再去做。

（9）我们学校__________有很多饭馆和便利店。

3. 看图片用存现句写句子。Make existential sentences according to the pictures.

（1）桌子上__________________

（2）黑板前_______________

（3）架子上__________________

（4）门口_________________

（5）楼上____________________

（6）前面_________________

4. 改错句。Correct the sentences.

（1）我买了很多东西，用花了很多钱。

____

（2）老师对不起，我会稍微几分钟迟到。

____

（3）明天要考试，我稍微一点儿担心。

____

（4）我和朋友一起合租电费。

____

（5）我去学校食堂买一套饭。

____

5. 完成句子。Complete the sentences.

（1）同学们在图书馆__________。（不是……就是……）

（2）A：你们的学校怎么样？

B：__________。（可）

（3）他送了我一盒巧克力，我__________。（可）

（4）我租的房子一个月 1000 块，__________。（算）

（5）我和他吃过一次饭，__________。（算）

（6）A：你觉得你幸运吗？

B：__________。（算）

（7）你说得太快了，我听不懂，__________。（稍微）

（8）他不知道广东菜，__________。（更不用说）

（9）我没见过他，__________。（更不用说）

6. 根据课文回答问题。Answer the questions according to the text.

课文 1

（1）艾文现在住哪儿？他的房子怎么样？

___

（2）他是怎么找房子的？

___

课文 2

（1）“我”的朋友为什么不能睡懒觉了？

___

（2）他每天怎么来学校？

___

（3）除了交通方便，公寓周围的环境怎么样？生活方便吗？

___

（4）公寓住着舒服吗？为什么？

___

（5）公寓的租金贵吗？为什么？

___

7. 租房知多少。What do you know about renting?

（1）你知道哪些和租房有关的词语？说一说下面词语的意思。

<table>
<tr>
<td>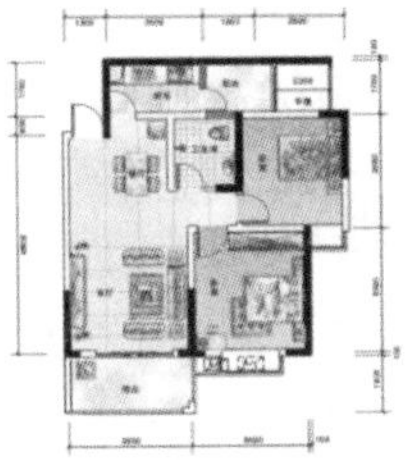
hùxíngtú
户型图
house type image</td>
<td>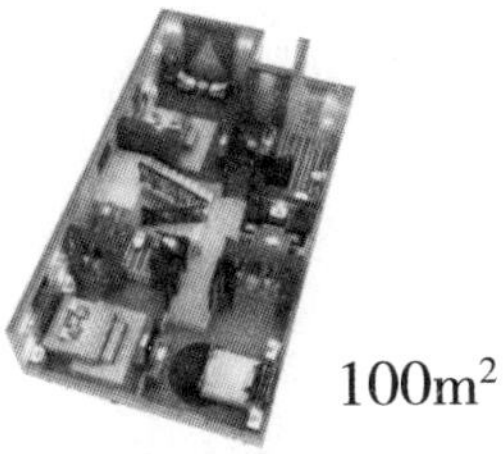
miànjī
面积
dwelling area</td>
<td>
cháoxiàng
朝向
orientations</td>
</tr>
<tr>
<td>
zhōngjiè
中介
intermediary agent</td>
<td>
yājīn
押金
guarantee deposit</td>
<td>
hé tóng
合 同
contract</td>
</tr>
</table>

（2）租房子的时候，下面的词语中，你会最先考虑哪一个，最后考虑哪一个？给它们排一排顺序，说一说为什么。

环境　交通　朝向　租金　面积　楼层　电梯　物业

最先考虑——→最后考虑

____

____

____

（3）天才中介。

全班同学分为若干组，其中几组是中介公司的业务员，其他同学是“要租房子的人”，可以是朋友、一家人等关系，例如：

租客	租客情况
客户 1	一个学生，需要离学校近，安静的学习环境，没有车
客户 2	两个女生，刚刚工作，工作比较忙，有时加晚班
客户 3	一位老板，刚结婚，做生意，有车
客户 4	一家人，爸妈、奶奶、孩子，奶奶 70 多岁，孩子刚上小学

老师将几份出租房信息（纸质、租房 App 链接都可）随机发给业务员，业务员自由走动寻找客户，为客户介绍不同的出租房，客户根据需要选择自己满意的出租房，交易成功最多的业务员赢。

练习对话时，尽可能多地使用下面的词语和句式：

参考词语	中介、合租、套、平方米、卧室、客厅、厨房、阳台、宽敞、空气流通、周围、便利、地段、租金、费、挑剔、谨慎……
参考句式	算……，不算…… 不是……就是…… ……得很 稍微有点儿…… ……，更不用说……

8．小练笔。Writing.

你要出国留学两年，想把房子租给别人，请写一个“有意思”的租房广告。（不少于100个字）

房 屋 出 租

第五课　中国的高铁真方便

China's high-speed rail is so convenient

课前热身 Warming up

你的国家有高铁吗？你坐过中国的高铁吗？

Does your country have high-speed rail? Have you ever taken a high-speed rail in China?

生词 New words

1	高铁	gāotiě	名	high-speed rail
2	新闻	xīnwén	名	news
3	了不起	liǎobuqǐ	形	extraordinary; amazing
4	公里	gōnglǐ	量	kilometer
5	窗子	chuāngzi	名	window

6	景色	jǐngsè	名	scenery; view; landscape
7	稳	wěn	形	steady; stable; firm
8	另外	lìngwài	代/副/连	other; in addition; besides
9	刚好	gānghǎo	形/副	just; exactly; happen to
10	窗口	chuāngkǒu	名	window; wicket
11	取票	qǔ piào		to take a ticket
12	取票机	qǔ piào jī		ticket machine
13	目前	mùqián	名	at present; at the moment
14	网站	wǎngzhàn	名	website
15	热爱	rè'ài	动	to ardently love; to have deep love for
16	事物	shìwù	名	thing; matter
17	世界	shìjiè	名	world
18	准时	zhǔnshí	形	punctual; on time
19	候车	hòuchē	动	to wait for a bus or train
20	走廊	zǒuláng	名	corridor; passage
21	好像	hǎoxiàng	动	to seem; to be like
22	瘦	shòu	形	thin; lean
23	尝试	chángshì	动	to try; to attempt
24	点餐	diǎn cān		to order a meal
25	扶手	fúshǒu	名	handrail; armrest
26	送餐	sòng cān		to deliver of meal
27	当时	dāngshí	名	then; at that time

28	改签	gǎi qiān		to rebook
29	退票	tuìpiào	动	to return the ticket

专名 Proper nouns

深圳*	Shēnzhèn	Shenzhen (a city's name)

课文 Text

课文1 Text 1

阿里：来中国以前，看新闻说中国的高铁很了不起，所以上个周末我体验了一次。

米亚：去了哪儿？

阿里：深圳。从广州到深圳，你猜要多长时间？

米亚：以前我坐汽车去深圳，要两个多小时。高铁应该要一个小时吧？

阿里：不对，最快的只要二十九分钟。

米亚：这么快？

阿里：是啊，高铁的速度是每小时 300 多公里，给你看我拍的视频。

…………

米亚：哇，太快了！窗子外面的景色像飞起来了一样。不过，这么快的速度，你不觉得难受吗？

阿里：完全不会。高铁又快又稳，座位很宽敞，坐着很舒服，另外，车上的服务也非常好。

米亚：听你这么说，我也很想体验一下。刚好假期我打算去北京，要怎么买票？

阿里：你可以提前在网上买票，出发前去车站的窗口用护照取票就行。

米亚：我们不能在取票机取票吗？

阿里：目前，外国人还不能用取票机。

米亚：好吧。对了，你能发给我买票的网站吗？

阿里：没问题，我现在就发。

课文❷ Text 2

我有一个朋友，特别热爱新鲜事物。他听说中国的高铁是世界上最快的高铁之一，所以来中国以后，每次旅行都会选择坐高铁。跟飞机相比，高铁非常准时，而且不用提前两个小时去车站候车。最重要的是，因为他是个大个子，高铁的座位比较大，走廊宽敞，让他非常满意。他开玩笑地说："坐高铁的时候，我觉得自己好像瘦了。"

最近一次坐高铁，他还尝试了高铁上的自助点餐。用手机扫一下座位扶手上的二维码，然后选择喜欢的食物，下单、付款，服务员就会送餐到你的座位上，是不是特别方便？

他虽然坐过很多次高铁，很少迟到，但还是有几次没赶上。他说当时一点儿也不担心，因为改签或者退票都很方便。他对中国的高铁非常满意，甚至可以说来中国不坐高铁，就跟没来中国一样。

语言知识 Language guidelines

知识1 Tip 1

“了不起”

“中国的高铁很了不起”

形容词“了不起”的意思是大大超过寻常，很突出。修饰名词时必须加“的”；作谓语时，前面常加“真”“太”“多么”等，表示感叹语气。例如：

The adjective “了不起” means something is very unusual or remarkable. When it modifies a noun, it must be followed “的”. When it is the predicate in a sentence, it is often preceded by “真”, “太”, “多么”, etc., to express exclamation. E. g.,

(1) 贝多芬是一位了不起的音乐家。

(2) 他能说好几种语言，真了不起！

(3) 中国的长城已经几千年了，太了不起了！

知识2 Tip 2

“另外”

“高铁又快又稳，座位很宽敞，坐着很舒服，另外，车上的服务也非常好。”

1. 副词“另外”表示所说的范围之外，放在句中，常和“还”“再”“又”等副词一起用。例如：

The adverb “另外” means that something is beyond the mentioned scope, and is often used in conjunction with adverbs such as "还", "再" and "又" when placed in the middle of the sentence. E. g.,

(1) 会议快开始了，我们另外做 PPT 来不及，就用以前的吧！

(2) 昨天逛街，他买了一件衣服，另外还买了一双鞋。

(3) 这个游戏要 4 个人，现在 3 个人不够，你另外再找一个人。

(4) 我们点了几盘菜，他又另外点了一份饺子。

2. 连词“另外”有“此外”的意思，一般连接小句、句子或者段落。例如：

The conjunction "另外" means "in addition" and is usually used to connect clauses, sentences, or paragraphs. E. g.,

(1) 我给他打了电话，另外又发了微信。

(2) 我哥哥中文说得很流利，交了不少中国朋友，另外，他的汉字写得也很不错。

(3) 我朋友喜欢高铁，他说高铁的座位比较宽敞，很舒服。另外，上次在高铁上他还用 App 点餐，方便得很。

知识3 Tip 3

教学视频

“刚好”

“刚好假期我打算去北京”

副词“刚好”比“正好”更带强调意味，强调就在那个时间点上，即时间不早不晚、空间不前不后、数量不多不少，常用于口语。“刚好”后可以加动词或形容词，也可以用在有数量词的句子或放在主语前。例如：

More emphatic than “正好”, “刚好” is commonly used in colloquial Chinese to denote that something is perfectly balanced or becoming to a particular situation in terms of timing, place or quantity. “刚好” can not only be followed by a verb or an adjective, but also be used in a sentence with a numeral-classifier compound or in front of the subject. E. g. ,

(1) 我到教室的时候，他们也刚好到。

(2) 这双鞋子不大不小，刚好合适。

(3) 在这儿刚好能看见学校的操场。

(4) 刚好我有两张电影票，我们可以一起去看。

练习 Exercises

1. **词语消消乐**。Play the words game.

体验	改签	座位	高铁
事物	准时	速度	候车
服务	新鲜	窗口	点餐
尝试	满意	取票	选择

例如：新鲜事物*

____________　____________　____________

____________　____________　____________

____________　____________　____________

2. **选词填空**。Choose the right words to fill in the blanks.

了不起　刚好　座位　选择　准时　好像　尝试　稳

（1）因为我喜欢中国文化，所以我__________来中国学习中文。

（2）成功的第一步就是努力去__________。

（3）我们班的同学互相关心、互相帮助，__________一家人。

（4）我们到车站时__________赶上那班公共汽车。

（5）老板，我们一共 8 个人，店里还有__________吗？

（6）明天上午九点，我们__________从学校东门出发。

（7）我第一次滑冰，站不__________，经常摔倒。

（8）他只学了一年的中文就通过了 HSK 4 级，真__________！

3. **改错句**。Correct the sentences.

（1）服务员对我们说，你要点餐什么？

____

（2）高铁票可以买在取票机。

____

* 搭配的词语意思合理即可，所给的词语可重复使用。

（3）篮球比赛的票我去取票。

____

（4）我能不能尝试你的新手机？

____

（5）我坐在窗口座位上。

____

（6）另外我学习中文，我也学习英文。

____

（7）他不仅高个子，还很帅。

____

（8）爸爸今天不能来，他太忙了，要做很多事物。

____

（9）每个人都热爱他的家人。

____

4. 组句。Rearrange the words to form a sentence.

（1）分钟　从　深圳　二十九　只要　广州　到

____

（2）速度　高铁　公里　的　是　300 多　每小时

____

（3）的　像　景色　一样　了　窗外　飞起来

____

（4）护照　去　要用　车站　外国人　窗口　取票

____

（5）车站　两小时　去　提前　你　候车　不用

____

（6）满意　的　座位　他　高铁　对　非常

____

5．完成句子。Complete the sentences.

（1）A：你觉得在中国的生活怎么样？

B：________________________________。（满意）

（2）今天的晚会________________________________。（准时）

（3）他是我们班最______________________________。（之一）

（4）____________________，现在大家都在看手机。（以前）

（5）我买了两本小说，________________________。（另外）

（6）我________________________，有时间陪你去。（刚好）

（7）____________________，你的中文好多了。（跟……相比）

（8）昨天他说他马上就回国了，____________________。（当时）

6．根据课文回答问题。Answer the questions according to the text.

课文 1

（1）为什么高铁窗外的景色像飞起来了一样？

____

（2）高铁的速度有多快？

____

（3）除了高铁的速度以外，阿里还喜欢高铁的什么？

____

（4）怎么买高铁票？外国人取票时要注意什么？

____

课文 2

（1）“我”的朋友在中国旅行时会选择什么交通方式？为什么？

____

（2）在高铁上怎么点餐？

____

（3）没赶上高铁时，“我”的朋友为什么一点儿也不担心？

____

7. 中国小调查。Finish a survey about China.

（1）说一说各种交通方式的优点和缺点。

交通方式	优点	缺点
高铁		
飞机		
汽车		
自行车		

（2）你知道中国的“新四大发明”吗？看相关视频，说一说它们在你的生活中有什么作用。

 高铁 High-speed rail	 支付宝 Alipay
 共享单车 Shared bikes	 网购 Online shopping

（3）上面的“新四大发明”中，如果你得放弃一个，你会选择放弃哪个发明？如果可以再加一个新的“发明”，你会加什么？为什么？

8．小练笔。Writing.

我来中国有一段时间了，我觉得中国跟我以前想的不一样……(不少于100个字)

第六课　坐飞机

Take a plane

课前热身 Warming up

你坐过飞机吗？坐上飞机前你还做了哪些事情？

Have you ever taken a plane? What else did you do before getting on the plane?

生词 New words

1	小姐	xiǎojiě	名	young lady; Miss
2	登机	dēng jī		to board a plane
3	手续	shǒuxù	名	procedures; formalities
4	国际	guójì	形/名	international; internation

5	区	qū	名	area; district; region; an administrative diveision
6	航空	hángkōng	动	aviation; navigate by air
7	柜台	guìtái	名	counter
8	先生	xiānsheng	名	mister (Mr.); gentleman; sir
9	把	bǎ	介	used to put the object is placed before the verb which is the recipient of the action
10	托运	tuōyùn	动	to check in luggage
11	传送带	chuánsòngdài	名	conveyor belt
12	箱子	xiāngzi	名	case; box
13	充电宝	chōngdiànbǎo	名	Charge Pal; power bank
	充电	chōngdiàn	动	to charge (a battery)
14	打火机	dǎhuǒjī	名	lighter
15	电池	diànchí	名	cell; battery
16	超过	chāoguò	动	to exceed; to surpass; to outstrip
17	重新	chóngxīn	副	again; anew; afresh
18	登机牌	dēng jī pái		boarding pass; boarding check

19	安检	ānjiǎn	动	security check
20	登机口	dēng jī kǒu		boarding gate
21	空姐	kōngjiě	名	airline stewardess; air hostess
22	空少	kōng shào		airline steward
23	糊涂	hútu	形	muddled; confused
24	拦	lán	动	to bar; to block the way
25	发现	fāxiàn	动	to find; to notice; to discover; to realize
26	照相机	zhàoxiàngjī	名	camera
27	害怕	hàipà	动	to be afraid; to fear; to be scared
28	候机室	hòu jī shì		airport lounge or waiting room
	候机	hòu jī		to wait for the flight
29	广播	guǎngbō	动/名	to broadcast; (radio) broadcast
30	忽然	hūrán	副	suddenly; all of a sudden
31	抱歉*	bàoqiàn	形	be sorry; apologetic
32	由于	yóuyú	介/连	owing to; due to; because; since
33	临时	línshí	副/形	at the time when sth. happens; temporary; for a short time

34	取消	qǔxiāo	动	to cancel; to abolish
35	心情	xīnqíng	名	mood; frame of mind
36	透	tòu	动/形	to pass through; fully; thoroughly

专名 Proper nouns

中国南方航空*	Zhōngguó nánfāng hángkōng	China Southern Airlines

课文 Text

课文1 Text 1

（在机场服务台）

阿　里：小姐，你好，请问在哪儿办理登机手续？

服务员：您是国际航班还是国内航班？

阿　里：我是国际航班。

服务员：国际航班在 A 区。请问，您的票是哪家航空公司的呢？

阿　里：中国南方航空公司。

服务员：请稍等，我帮您查一下……您得去 H 柜台办理登机手续。

阿　里：好的，谢谢！

…………

（在航空公司柜台）

服务员：先生，请把您的护照给我。

阿　里：好的。

服务员：请您把要托运的行李放在传送带上。请问，箱子里有充电宝、打火机、电池吗？

阿　里：没有。

服务员：先生，免费托运的行李不能超过 20 公斤，现在 22 公斤。

阿　里：啊，真的吗？那我拿点东西出来吧！

（阿里把给家人买的礼物拿出来，把大衣穿在身上，再把行李箱重新放到传送带上。）

服务员：现在可以了。请问，您选择靠窗的座位还是靠走廊的座位？

阿　里：靠窗的。

服务员：好的。这是您的登机牌，请去 A 区安检，然后在 16 号登机口登机。

阿　里：谢谢！

课文 2 Text 2

我特别喜欢选择坐飞机出行，因为飞机又快又舒服，而且飞机上的空姐、空少服务也十分周到。不过，我每次坐飞机都不那么顺利，总是会做点儿糊涂事儿，不是忘记带护照，就是起床起晚了，赶不上飞机。还有一次，托运行李的时候，工作人员说我的行李有问题，把我的箱子拦了下来，检查了半天，最后发现是照相机的电池没有拿出来。

不过，这些事情我都不害怕，我最害怕的是在候机室，等了很久，机场的广播忽然说："对不起，我们十分抱歉地通知您，由于天气的原因，今天的航班临时取消了。"那个时候的心情真是糟糕透了，因为取消以后，还得改签或者重新买票，不过有什么办法呢？我得回家呀。

语言知识 Language guidelines

知识1 Tip 1

“把”字句₁

“请把您的护照给我”“请您把要托运的行李放在传送带上。”“再把行李箱重新放到传送带上”

这一类的“把”字句主要用来表达通过某动作使某事物发生一定的变化，如位置的移动、所属关系的转移、状态的改变等，由“在”“到”“给”“成”加宾语充当其他成分，格式如“主语＋把＋宾语＋动词＋在/到/给/成……”。

The “把” sentence is mainly used to present the alteration of something by an action in terms of position, ownership, state, etc. The object is placed right after “把” in the usual sentence structure. However, certain verbs can take two objects, and prepositions such as “在”“到”“给” and “成” are involved. The structure of the “把” sentence with two objects is “subject + 把 + direct object + verb + 在/到/给/成 + indirect object”.

其中，“把…… + 动词 + 在/到……”常表示事物位置的变化。例如：

“把……＋verb＋在/到……” often indicates a change in the position of something. E. g. ,

（1）我把行李箱放在传送带上了。

（2）你别把书包放到地上。

(3) 妈妈忘记把钥匙放到包里了。

“把…… + 动词 + 给……”常表示事物位置的变化或所属关系的转移。例如：

“把…… + verb + 给……” often indicates a change in the position or ownership of something. E. g. ,

(1) 我把作业交给老师。

(2) 她想把这件礼物送给朋友。

(3) 你能把昨天的照片发给我吗?

“把…… + 动词 + 成……”常表示事物状态的改变。例如：

“把…… + verb + 成……” often indicates a change in the state of something. E. g. ,

(1) 他把这本英文小说翻译成了中文。

(2) 你不应该把“干”写成“千”。

(3) 我把 1 号登机口听成了 7 号登机口。

知识 2 Tip 2

“忽然”

“广播忽然说”

副词“忽然”表示情况发生得迅速而又出人意料。例如：

The adverbs “忽然” means that things happen quickly and unexpectedly. E. g. ,

（1）老师忽然不说话了。

（2）刚才天气不错，现在忽然下起雨来。

（3）我们在聊天，忽然有人敲门。

用法对比："忽然"和"突然"

Compare："忽然" and "突然"

作为副词的"忽然"和"突然"意思相同，一般可以换用，但"突然"比"忽然"更强调情况发生得迅速和出人意料。"忽然"很少用在主语前。此外，"突然"还是形容词，而"忽然"只有副词的用法。例如：

The adverbs "忽然" and "突然" have the same meaning, which can be used interchangeably in most cases. However, "突然" emphasizes the rapid and unexpected occurrence of a situation compared to "忽然". "忽然" is seldom used in front of the subject. In addition, "突然" is also an adjective, while "忽然" is only used as an adverb. E. g. ,

（1）这件事情太突然了。（＊忽然）

（2）因为突然的大雪，很多航班临时取消了。（＊忽然）

（3）他走得很突然，谁也没有告诉，就回国了。（＊忽然）

知识3 Tip 3

"由于"

"由于天气的原因，今天的航班临时取消了。"

"由于"表示原因。"由于"作介词，可以出现在"是"后面，也可以放在主语的前面或后面。"由于"作连词，后一小句开头可以用

“所以”“因此”“因而”。例如：

“由于” is used to introduce the cause. As a preposition, “由于” can stand after “是” or either side of the subject. When “由于” functions as a conjunction, “所以”, “因此” or “因而” can be used at the beginning of the latter clause. E. g. ,

(1) 他能考100分，完全是由于自己的努力。

(2) 我由于工作的原因，需要来中国学习一年中文。

(3) 由于签证没有办好，因此我们改变了旅游的计划。

用法对比：“由于”和“因为”

Compare: “由于” and “因为”

口语里用“因为”较多，较少用“由于”。连词“由于”可以和“因此”“因而”一起用，“因为”不能。连词“因为”可以用在后一小句，连词“由于”不能。例如：

In the spoken language, “由于” is less commonly used than “因为”. The conjunction “由于” can be used together with “因此” or “因而”, but “因为” cannot; “因为” can be used in the latter clause, but “由于” cannot. E. g. ,

(1) 由于他学习努力，因此得到老师的表扬。(* 因为他学习努力)

他得到老师的表扬，是因为他学习努力。(* 由于他学习努力)

(2) 由于台风来了，因此飞机不能起飞。(* 因为台风来了)

飞机不能起飞，因为台风来了。(* 由于台风来了)

知识4 Tip 4

“临时”

“今天的航班临时取消了。”

1. 副词“临时”表示当事情快发生的时候。例如：

The adverb “临时” indicates that something is about to happen. E. g. ,

(1) 你应该早点复习，现在快考试了，你临时着急也没用。

(2) 原来想打的回去，突然发现附近风景很美，临时决定走路回去。

(3) 我去拿快递，没想到包裹又大又重，临时找了保安帮忙。

2. 形容词“临时”还有“短期的，暂时”的意思。例如：

The adjective “临时” also means “temporarily, for the time being”. E. g. ,

(1) 下雨了，我临时借用朋友的伞回家。

(2) 没有杯子了，我们临时拿碗来喝水。

(3) 天气不好，学校的运动会临时取消。

知识5 Tip 5

“透了”

“那个时候的心情真是糟糕透了”

“透了”表示程度极深，多用于贬义，用在动词、形容词后，中间不能加“得”“不”。例如：

“透了” indicates a great extent and is often used in a negative way. When it is used after a verb or an adjective, “得” or “不” cannot be added in the middle. E. g.,

(1) 那个人真是坏透了。

(2) 我恨透了偷我手机的人。

(3) 我的东西太多，搬家真是麻烦透了。

练习 Exercises

1. **看图片写词语**。Write words according to the pictures.

(1) ____________

(2) ____________

(3) ____________

(4) ____________

(5) ____________

(6) ____________

（7）________

（8）________

（9）________

（10）________

（11）________

（12）________

（13）________

（14）________

（15）________

2. 词语搭配。Complete the phrases.

办理________	重新________	托运________
超过________	国际________	取消________
忽然________	害怕________	临时________

3. **选词填空**。Choose the right words to fill in the blanks.

害怕 糊涂 心情 服务 手续 忽然 安检 由于 托运

(1) 你好，请问你有哪些行李需要________？

(2) 你知道办签证的________吗？

(3) ________不好的时候，我常听他的歌。

(4) 我真________，忘记把钥匙拔下来了。

(5) 这家航空公司的________是最好的。

(6) 我________想起来，我的书包还在教室里。

(7) 小孩子都非常________看医生。

(8) 把打火机扔了吧，机场________的时候不可以带。

(9) ________下大雨，运动会临时取消了。

4. **"把"字句挑战赛**。Make "把" sentences as required.

(1) 看图片，写"把"字句。

a. 把__________在______

b. 把__________在______

c. 把__________到_____

d. 把__________到_____

e. 把__________给_____

f. 把__________给_____

g. 把__________成_____

h. 把__________成_____

（2）拼“把”字句。

全班分为若干组，6 或 7 人一组，每组选一个组长。老师将能拼成正确的“把”字句的词卡随机发给组员，组员合作拼出正确的“把”字句。每组需完成 4 或 5 个“把”字句。拼对一个“把”字句后，组长指挥组员摆出一个造型，然后组长拍照，小组前后的造型不能重复。全部句子拼对，同时摆造型和拍照用时最少的小组赢。

5. 改错句。Correct the sentences.

(1) 我们很快登机飞机了。

____

(2) 明天不上课，我们都开心透了。

____

(3) 他不能来上课，由于生病了。

____

(4) 我一进教室就放书包在桌上。

____

(5) 我寄那个快递给你了。

____

(6) 我不小心写“午饭”成“牛饭”了。

____

(7) 我觉得你把钱不能借给他。

____

(8) 我把教室的钥匙还没还给阿姨。

____

6. 完成句子。Complete the sentences.

(1) 他好像喝了酒，警察______________________________。(拦)

(2) 奶奶今年 80 多岁了，__________________________。(糊涂)

(3) 刚才天气还不错，______________________________。(忽然)

(4) ______________________________，我不能陪你去了。(由于)

(5) 今天别跟我说话，我的心情______________________。(透了)

(6) 你刚才说什么我没听见，________________________。(重新)

（7）听到妈妈生病了，________________。（临时）

（8）班长买了蛋糕，但忘了买盘子，____________。（临时）

7. 根据课文回答问题。 Answer the questions according to the text.

课文 1

（1）阿里坐飞机去国内还是国外？

____

（2）登机以前需要办理哪些手续？

____

（3）阿里为什么要从行李箱里拿点东西出来？

____

课文 2

（1）"我"为什么选择坐飞机出行？

____

（2）"我"为什么每次坐飞机都不太顺利？

____

（3）坐飞机的时候，"我"最害怕什么？为什么？

____

8．**机场挑战赛**。Situational dialogues in the airport.

（1）看图片，完成对话。

A：______________________

B：______________________

A：______________________

B：______________________

A：______________________

B：______________________

A：______________________

B：______________________

（2）“逃离”机场。

全班学生分为三类：机场工作人员、普通乘客、要“逃离”机场的人。老师将三类“身份卡”随机发给学生，并公开所有的身份，但是每位学生只能看自己的身份，不能互看身份。

参考身份	
机场工作人员	柜台服务员、安检员、警察、空姐……
普通乘客	耳朵听不清楚的老人、赶时间的老板、行李超重的留学生、带孩子的妈妈、带宠物的主人、独自登机的小孩子……

机场工作人员公开身份，并开始“工作”。其他同学通过表演展示身份，如“耳朵听不清楚的老人”听不清楚别人的话，“赶时间的老板”很没有耐心……要“逃离”机场的人没有身份，需要自己设计身份，并在表演过程中说完3个“把”字句。

如果要“逃离”机场的人说完3个“把”字句并顺利登机，则逃离成功，其他人受到惩罚；相反，如果要“逃离”机场的人没有说完3个“把”字句，或在登机前被找出，则逃离失败，受到惩罚。

练习对话时，要尽可能地多使用下面的词语和句式。

参考词语	登机、手续、国际、国内、区、航空、登机牌、托运、安检、安检口、传送带、超过、重新、候机、候机室、广播、抱歉、取消……
参考句式	把…… 由于……原因，……

9. 小练笔。Writing.

我第一次坐飞机的时候……（不少于100个字）

第七课　学做中国菜

Learn to make Chinese food

课前热身 Warming up

你知道哪些中国菜？你会做吗？

What Chinese food do you know? Can you cook it?

生词 New words

1	干什么	gàn shénme		what to do
2	道	dào	名/量	road; way; a measure word used for order, questions, etc.; a measure word used for courses in a meal, stages

				in a procedure, etc.
3	炒	chǎo	动	to stir-fry; to sauté
4	材料	cáiliào	名	material; data
5	摆	bǎi	动	to put; to place; to arrange
6	咦*	yí	叹	(used to express surprise) well; why
7	绿色	lǜsè	形	green
8	葱	cōng	名	shallot
9	盐	yán	名	salt
10	接着	jiēzhe	动/副	to follow; to carrying on
11	去皮	qù pí		to remove the peel
12	切	qiē	动	to cut; to slice
13	散	sàn	动	to break up; to disperse; to dispel; to let out
14	葱花	cōnghuā	名	chopped shallot
15	锅	guō	名	pot; pan
16	鸡蛋液	jī dàn yè		egg liquid
	液	yè		liquid; fluid
17	盛	chéng	动	to fill; to ladle
18	复杂	fùzá	形	complicated; complex
19	做法	zuòfǎ	名	way of doing or making a thing
20	于是	yúshì	连	thereupon; as a result
21	动手	dòngshǒu	动	to start work

22	手艺	shǒuyì	名	workmanship; handicraft
23	难不倒	nán bù dǎo		not to pose a problem for sb
24	勺子	sháozi	名	spoon
25	舀	yǎo	动	to spoon up
26	咸	xián	形	salty; salted
27	菜谱	càipǔ	名	cookbook; menu
28	少许	shǎoxǔ	形	a little; a few
29	适量	shìliàng	形	appropriate amount
30	模糊	móhu	形	indistinct; blurred; dim; vague
31	到底	dàodǐ	动/副	to the end; at last; after all; used in a question for emphasis
32	调味料	tiáowèi liào		seasoning; flavouring
	调味	tiáowèi	动	to season; to flavour
33	淡	dàn	形	without enough salt; light; pale
34	那么	nàme	代/连	like that; then; in that case
35	等于	děngyú	动	to equal to; to be tantamount to

课文 Text

课文1 Text 1

米　亚：你在干什么？

王乐乐：我打算做一道简单又美味的中国菜——西红柿炒鸡蛋！

米　亚：哇，太棒了！需要哪些材料？

王乐乐：你看，都摆在这儿。

米　亚：两个西红柿，四个鸡蛋……咦？这个绿色的叫什么？

王乐乐：啊，这个叫葱。我们还要准备一点儿盐。

米　亚：我去拿。

…………

米　亚：现在东西都准备好了，接着怎么做？

王乐乐：先用热水把西红柿烫一下，去皮，然后再把它切成小块，把鸡蛋打散后，加一点儿盐，最后再把葱切成葱花。

米　亚：我试试……这样切对吧？

王乐乐：对。接着把油倒在锅里，油热了以后，再把鸡蛋液倒进去，炒一炒就盛出来。

米　亚：这就是炒鸡蛋吧，然后呢？

王乐乐：然后把西红柿倒进去，放点盐炒一炒，再把鸡蛋倒进去，接着和西红柿一起炒，最后放点葱花就做好了。

米　亚：听起来有点复杂，这次我看你做，下次我自己再试一试。

课文2 Text 2

周末朋友给我做了一道西红柿炒鸡蛋，味道好，做法也不难。于是我想自己动手做一次，请朋友尝尝我的手艺。

去皮、切菜、打鸡蛋，这些都难不倒我，最难的是我不知道该放多少盐。朋友说放一点儿，我用勺子舀了一点儿盐，她说太多了，我倒回去一点儿，朋友又说太少了，于是我又加了一点儿盐，结果炒出来的菜咸了。

我跟着中文菜谱学做中国菜的时候，也常常遇到这样的问题：菜谱上常写着“一点儿”“少许”“适量”，可是这些词的意思都很模糊，我不知道到底应该放多少调味料？我做的菜不是太咸就是太淡，不是太甜就是没有味道。

我问中国朋友：“‘一点儿’到底是多少？”

她说：“‘一点儿’就是一点点。”

“‘少许’是多少？”

“‘少许’就是一点儿。”

“那么‘适量’是多少？”

“不多不少，刚刚好。”

说了等于没说。聪明的你知道吗？

语言知识 Language guidelines

知识❶ Tip 1

“干”

“你在干什么？”

1. 动词“干”有“做事”和“担任或从事某种工作”的意思。例如：

The verb “干” means “to do something” and “to do or engage in a certain kind of work”. E. g. ,

（1）这些事咱们今天要干完。

（2）刚毕业，我还不知道自己适合干什么。

（3）A：你以前干过哪些工作，怎么知道这么多？

B：我干过司机、干过导游，现在这些都不干了，开了家小公司。

2. 在口语中，“干什么”也常说成“干吗”，常用来询问原因或目的。注意，询问客观事物的道理时，只能用“为什么”或“怎么”，不能用“干什么”或“干吗”。例如：

In spoken Chinese, “干什么” is also often referred to as “干吗”, inquiring about the reason or purpose. It is noteworthy that when asking about the reason of objective things, only “为什么” or “怎么” can be used, instead of “干什么” or “干吗”. E. g. ,

（1）你去那么早干什么？

（2）我们只去玩两天，你带这么多行李干什么？

（3）干什么不回微信？我有急事找你啊！

（4）天空为什么是蓝色的？（*干什么）

（5）西瓜怎么长得这么大？（*干什么）

知识2 Tip 2

“接着”

“东西都准备好了，接着怎么做?”“接着和西红柿一起炒”

“接着”表示继续之前的事物或活动，后常带动词或名词。例如：

“接着” means to continue something or an activity. It is often followed by verbs or nouns. E. g. ,

（1）我们接着刚才的课文讲下去。

（2）吃完饭，接着做作业。

（3）上课了，同学们一个接着一个走进教室。

用法对比：“接着”和“继续”

Compare：“接着” and “继续”

“接着”和“继续”都有将活动连下去的意义。“继续”前后的人或事要一致，而“接着”前后既可以是同一个人或事物，也可以是不同的人或事物。“接着”一般也不单独作谓语。例如：

“接着” and “继续” both have the meaning of continuing the activity. “继续” is used in the latter clause that shares the same subject with the former one, while “接着” is allowed to modify a different subject. In addition, “接着” is not usually used as a predicate alone. E. g. ,

（1）刚才下了一会儿雨，现在又接着下了。(继续)

（2）刮完风，接着下雨。(* 继续)

（3）你跑完，我接着跑。(* 继续)

（4）比赛还在继续着。(* 接着)

知识3 Tip 3

“把”字句$_2$

“用热水把西红柿烫一下”“把鸡蛋打散”“把鸡蛋液倒进去”

“把”字句的另一种用法是用来说明动作对某事物的处置方式，或是通过动作使某事物产生某种影响或造成某种结果，基本句式是“主语 + 把 + 宾语 + 动词 + 其他成分”。

Another usage of the “把” sentence is to describe the way an action deals with something, or to cause an impact or result through an action. The basic sentence pattern is “subject + 把 + object + verb + other components”.

“把”字句在使用时要注意下面几点：

When using the “把” sentence, we should pay attention to the following rules:

1. 主语一定是动作的发出者。例如：

The subject must be the agent of the action. E. g. ,

(1) 我把门关上了。

(2) 他把水杯拿给我。

(3) 爸爸把孩子送到学校。

2. 宾语是动词处置的对象，是说话人心中已经确定的，表现在句子中既可以是明指，前面常有“这”“那”等标记；也可以是暗指，即没有标记，但是宾语所指是说话人和听话人都已知的事物。例如：

The object is the recipient of the action of the verb, which is already determined in the speaker's mind. It can be clearly pointed out in the sentence by using some determiners like “这”, “那”, etc. It can also be implied without any marks, but the object referred to is known to both the speaker and the hearer. E. g. ,

(1) 我把那扇门关上。

(2) 他把红色的水杯拿给我。

(3) 请把书放在桌子上。(*请把一本书放在桌子上。)

(4) 爸爸把孩子送到学校。(*爸爸把一个孩子送到学校。)

3. 动词必须是及物动词，能使宾语发生某种变化，产生某种结果。一些不具有处置意义的动词，如“有”“是”“在”“知道”“喜欢”“觉得”等，不能用在“把”字句中。例如：

The verb must be a transitive one, the action of which can make the object change and produce a certain result. Some verbs that only describe the subject's behavior instead of indicating what happened to the object, such as “有”, “是”, “在”, “知道”, “喜欢”, “觉得”, etc. cannot be used in the “把” sentence. E. g. ,

(1) *我把一部新手机有了。→我有了一部新手机。

(2) *我把这个秘密知道了。→我知道了这个秘密。

(3) *我把中文很喜欢。→我很喜欢中文。

4. 动词后面一定要有其他成分，用来说明动作产生的结果。其他成分可以是动态助词“了”“着”、动词的宾语、补语（可能补语除外）、动词重叠等。例如：

There must be some other elements after the verb to indicate the result of the action, such as "了""着", an object of a verb, a complement (except for potential complements), or a reduplicated verb, etc. E. g.,

(1) *我把面条吃。→我把面条吃了。

(2) *你把门开。→你把门开着。

(3) *别把这个秘密告诉。→别把这个秘密告诉他。

(4) *妈妈还没把客厅打扫。→妈妈还没把客厅打扫干净。

(5) *老师让我们把练习写。→老师让我们把练习写(一)写。

注意:动词后面不能用可能补语。例如:

Note: potential complements cannot be used after verbs. E. g.,

(1) *我们把这三盘菜吃得完。→我们能把这三盘菜吃完。

(2) *我一个人把这台空调挪不动。→我一个人不能把这台空调挪动。

(3) *这件衣服这么脏,你把它洗得干净?→这件衣服这么脏,你能把它洗干净?

5. 否定副词"不""没"等或能愿动词"会""能"等要放在"把"字的前面。例如:

The negative adverbs such as "不" and "没" or modal verbs such as "会" and "能" should be placed before the word "把". E. g.,

(1) 那盘菜不好吃,我没把它吃完。

(2) 他很讨厌,不想把书还给我。

(3) 我能把这个秘密告诉他吗?

知识4 Tip 4

“于是”

“于是我想自己动手做一次。”

连词“于是”用于后一分句前，表示后一事是承接前一事，后一事往往是由前一事引起的。可用在主语前，也可用在主语后。例如：

The conjunction “于是” is used at the beginning of the latter clause to indicate that the latter event is the continuation of the former event, which is often caused by the former event. It can be used before or after the subject. E. g. ,

（1）我有点儿饿，于是想点外卖。

（2）看到大家都在复习，于是他也把书拿出来复习了。

（3）明天是他的生日，于是我们打算给他买一份生日礼物。

用法对比：“于是”和“所以”

Compare: “于是” and “所以”

“于是”和“所以”都能够表示因果关系，但“于是”更强调前后两件事在时间上的承接关系，后面不能是状态的描述；“所以”常常和“因为”一起强调明显的因果关系，后面可以是状态的描述。“于是”只能用在后一分句前；“所以”常用在后一分句前，但也可以用在前一分句前。例如：

Both “于是” and “所以” can express causality, but “于是” emphasizes the temporal continuity of the two events, and cannot be followed by the description of the state. “所以” often works with “因为” to emphasize a clear causal relationship, which can be followed by a description of the state. “于是” can only be used at the beginning of the last clause; “所以” is usually used at the beginning of the last clause, but it can also be used to introduce the first clause. E. g. ,

于是	所以
图书馆很安静，于是我常在那儿写作业。	图书馆很安静，所以我很喜欢那儿。
今天天气好，于是我们决定去逛街。	今天天气好，所以逛街的人特别多。
这家店人太多，于是我们去了另一家。	之所以去另一家，是因为这里人太多。

知识5 Tip 5

“到底”

“到底应该放多少调味料?”“‘一点儿’到底是多少?”

1. 副词“到底”用于疑问句，表示进一步追究，常用在动词、形容词或主语之前。例如：

The adverb “到底” is used in interrogative sentences to indicate further inquiry. It is commonly used before a verb, an adjective, or the subject. E. g. ,

(1) 他到底来不来?

(2) 这道菜到底该放多少盐?

(3) 你现在到底饿不饿?

（4）到底谁是哥哥谁是弟弟？

2. “到底”后加动词或者形容词，还表示经过较长过程最后出现某种结果。句子后必须加“了”或者其他表示“完成”的词语。例如：

Adding a verb or an adjective after “到底” also indicates that something has come about at the end of a long process. The sentence must ended with “了” or other words indicating completion. E. g. ,

（1）这本书到底看完了。

（2）我想了很久，到底明白了。

（3）老师不说话了，大家到底安静了。

练习 Exercises

1. 用所给词语描述图片内容。 Describe the pictures with the given words.

炒　切　锅　盛　舀　葱花　盐　去皮　勺子　打散　倒

（1）________

（2）________

（3）________

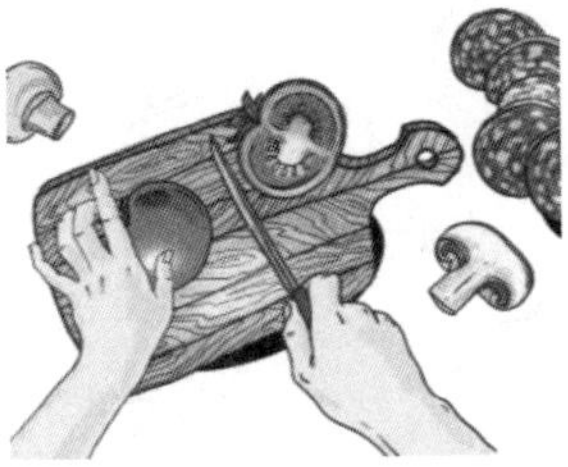

(4) ________　　(5) ________　　(6) ________

(7) ________　　(8) ________　　(9) ________

2. 词语搭配。Complete the phrases.

炒________　　准备________　　切________

盛________　　舀________　　________材料

少许________　　________复杂　　________模糊

3. 选词填空。Choose the right words to fill in the blanks.

准备	复杂	菜谱	做法	道	摆	适量	等于

(1) 不要想得那么________，这件事其实很简单。

(2) 妈妈让我把做好的菜________在桌子上。

（3）第一次做菜，我是看着__________做的。

（4）后天就考试了，我得好好__________。

（5）做这个菜，盐要__________，不然会太咸。

（6）你真笨，一加一__________几也不知道。

（7）我尝过一__________菜，味道很不错，可是名字我想不起来了。

（8）西红柿炒鸡蛋的__________很简单。

4. 用"把"字句描述图片内容。Describe the pictures with the "把" sentences.

（1）______________________

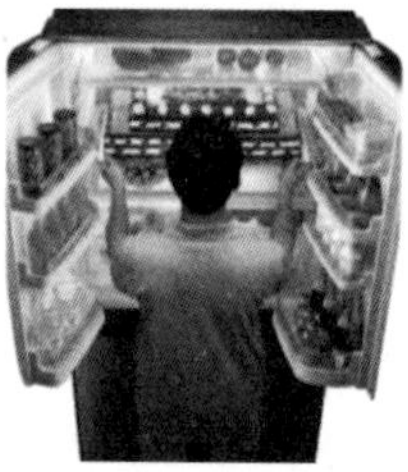

（2）______________________

（3）______________________

（4）______________________

(5) ______________________

(6) ______________________

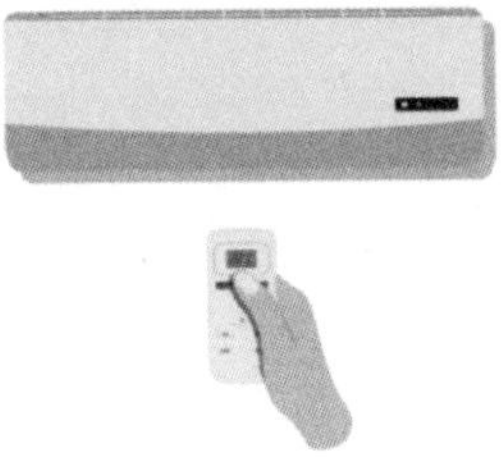

(7) ______________________

(8) ______________________

(9) ______________________

(10) ______________________

5. **改错句**。Correct the sentences.

(1) 先去皮苹果，然后切一下。

____

（2）我把一杯咖啡喝了。

____

（3）你把衣服洗。

____

（4）我把我的小狗喜欢。

____

（5）他把昨天的作业没做完。

____

（6）你把新衣服别弄脏了。

____

（7）他前天把高铁坐了去深圳。

____

6. 完成句子。Complete the sentences.

（1）刮风了，______________________________。（接着）

（2）我先说，______________________________。（接着）

（3）明天的考试______________________________。（准备）

（4）这个暑假______________________________。（准备）

（5）这份工作经常加班，______________________________。（于是）

（6）妈妈看见儿子回来了，______________________________。（于是）

（7）你每天都去那个地方，______________________________？（到底）

（8）一会儿说来，一会儿说不来，______________________________？（到底）

7. 根据课文回答问题。Answer the questions according to the text.

课文 1

（1）做西红柿炒鸡蛋需要哪些材料？

____

（2）这道菜的做法是什么？

____

课文 2

（1）"我"做的菜味道怎么样？为什么会这样？

____

（2）"我"学做中国菜的时候遇到了什么问题？

____

（3）"一点儿""少许""适量"的意思有什么不同？

____

8. 美食挑战赛。Exercises about food.

（1）完成下面的菜谱。

美味中文菜谱

【辣子鸡】

材料：

鸡肉（1 公斤）　　干辣椒（适量）

葱（少许）　　姜（1 块）

油（适量）　　盐（适量）

酱油（适量）　　料酒（适量）

做法：

①把材料______好；

②把材料洗______；

③把干辣椒用刀______成小段；

④把鸡肉用刀切成______；

⑤把盐、酱油和鸡肉______一起，腌（yān）半小时；

⑥把油倒在______；

⑦把鸡块炸成金黄色，然后______出来；

⑧再把油______在锅里；

⑨把干辣椒倒入，______一会儿；

⑩把鸡块倒入，加葱、姜一起______。

⑪把做好的辣子鸡______到盘子里。

（2）配音小游戏。

看一个做菜视频，然后老师关掉视频的声音，学生分组给视频配音，说的句子可以和视频里的不同，意思一样即可，全班评出最佳配音小组。

9．小练笔。Writing.

跟相同国家或地区的同学一起，介绍一道菜，可以用视频、图片、绘画、菜谱等方式介绍。（不少于 100 个字）

我们给大家介绍一道菜，名字叫＿＿＿＿＿＿＿＿＿＿＿＿＿＿＿＿，它的做法是＿＿＿＿＿＿＿＿＿＿＿＿＿＿＿＿＿＿＿＿＿＿＿＿＿＿＿＿

＿＿＿＿＿＿＿＿＿＿＿＿＿＿＿＿＿＿＿＿＿＿＿＿＿＿＿＿＿＿＿＿

＿＿＿＿＿＿＿＿＿＿＿＿＿＿＿＿＿＿＿＿＿＿＿＿＿＿＿＿＿＿＿＿

＿＿＿＿＿＿＿＿＿＿＿＿＿＿＿＿＿＿＿＿＿＿＿＿＿＿＿＿＿＿＿＿

＿＿＿＿＿＿＿＿＿＿＿＿＿＿＿＿＿＿＿＿＿＿＿＿＿＿＿＿＿＿＿＿

＿＿＿＿＿＿＿＿＿＿＿＿＿＿＿＿＿＿＿＿＿＿＿＿＿＿＿＿＿＿＿＿

＿＿＿＿＿＿＿＿＿＿＿＿＿＿＿＿＿＿＿＿＿＿＿＿＿＿＿＿＿＿＿＿

第八课　又到“双十一”

It’s double 11 again

课前热身 Warming up

你会网上购物吗？你知道“双十一”是什么吗？

Do you know how to shop online? Do you know what “Double Eleven” is?

生词 New words

1	购物节	gòu wù jié		shopping festival
2	网店	wǎngdiàn	名	online store
3	攻略	gōnglüè	名	strategy; guide
4	不然	bùrán	连	if not so; otherwise

5	被	bèi	介	used in a passive structure to introduce either the doer of the action, or the action alone
6	秒杀	miǎoshā	动	(Internet) to attend a flash sale; (sports or online game) to quickly defeat an opponent
7	秒	miǎo	量	second (unit of time)
8	购物车	gòu wù chē		shopping cart
9	凌晨	língchén	名	before dawn
10	只有……才……	zhǐyǒu……cái……		only if
11	此外	cǐwài	连	besides; in addition
12	货比三家	huò bǐ sān jiā		to shop around; to compare different offers
13	性价比	xìngjiàbǐ	名	cost-performance ratio
14	达人	dárén	名	intelligent; expert
15	经验	jīngyàn	名	experience
16	举行	jǔxíng	动	to hold (a meeting, ceremony, etc.)
17	促销	cùxiāo	动	to promote sales
18	各	gè	代/副	each; every; variously; respectively
19	电商	diànshāng	名	e-commerce

20	物美价廉	wù měi jià lián		good quality and cheap
21	不约而同	bùyuē'értóng		to do or think the same thing without prior consultation
22	仓库	cāngkù	名	warehouse
23	包裹	bāoguǒ	名	package
24	堆	duī	动/量	to pile up; to stack; pile
25	到处	dàochù	副	at all places; everywhere
26	忙碌	mánglù	形	busy
27	小哥	xiǎo gē		guy; man
28	冰箱	bīngxiāng	名	refrigerator
29	用不着	yòng bù zháo		do not need; have no use for; there is no need to
30	浪费	làngfèi	动	to waste
31	剁手*	duò shǒu		to go shopping

专名 Proper nouns

1	双十一	Shuāng shíyī	Double Eleven (November 11th)
2	黑色星期五	Hēisè xīngqī wǔ	Black Friday
3	天猫	Tiānmāo	Tmall

课文 Text

课文1 Text 1

米亚：我发现你最近总在逛淘宝，你要买什么东西？

阿里：你不知道吗？过几天就是“双十一”了。

米亚：“双十一”是什么？

阿里：有点儿像美国的“黑色星期五”，“双十一”是中国的购物节。每年的11月11日，淘宝上很多网店都会打折，这时候买东西特别划算。

米亚：你当天买就可以了，不用这么着急吧？

阿里：那可不行！得提前逛，做好攻略，不然东西都被别人抢光了。

米亚：有这么难买吗？

阿里：是啊，这叫“秒杀”，很多商品几秒钟就卖完了。

米亚：怎么“秒杀”呢？

阿里：提前选好想买的商品，把它加到购物车里，一到11月11日的凌晨就付钱，只有这样，才能抢到你想要的宝贝。

米亚：明白了。

阿里：此外，提前逛淘宝，还能货比三家，选到性价比最高的商品。

米亚：看来你是个“网购达人”啊！经验果然丰富。

阿里：经验丰富是丰富，不过也花了不少钱。好了，不说了，我要继续逛了。

课文 2 Text 2

2009 年 11 月 11 日，天猫举行了一场网上促销活动。后来，这一天变成了中国人的购物节，各家电商都会打折，平时需要支付运费的商品也会包邮。为了买到物美价廉的商品，很多人都会不约而同地在这一天网购。11 月 11 日之后的一段时间，每家快递公司的仓库里，包裹都堆得像山一样高，大街上、小区里到处都是忙碌的快递小哥和拿包裹的人。

上一次“双十一”我朋友买了一台冰箱，他说比实体店便宜了四百多块，打算今年再买一些东西，于是很早就开始做攻略了。去年我也买了不少，一些东西便宜是便宜，但是买来以后很多都用不着，也是一种浪费，所以今年“双十一”我不打算“剁手”了，你呢？

语言知识 Language guidelines

知识 1 Tip 1

教学视频

“被”字句

“不然东西都被别人抢光了”

“被”字句是表示被动的介词“被”“叫”“让”“给”及其宾语作状语，放在动词前表示被动意义的一种句式。“被”字句多数用来表达“不如意，不愉快”的意思。

The “被” sentence is a sentence pattern in which a preposition such as “被”, “叫”“让” or “给” and the object are used as an adverbial, and placed before the verb to convey the passive voice. The “被” sentence is mostly used to express the unpleasant mood.

其基本句式：

The basic sentence pattern：

主语＋被（叫/让/给）＋宾语＋动词＋其他成分 subject＋被（叫/让/给）＋object＋verb＋other elements

1. “被”字句的主语通常是明确的，其前大多也不用数量词修饰。例如：

The subject of the “被” sentence is generally definite, and most of them are not modified by a numeral-classifier compound. E. g. ,

（1）这个包裹被阿里取走了。

（2）我的电脑被他修好了。

（3）那个玩具被弟弟弄坏了。

2. 不需要强调施事者时，“被”字的宾语可以省略不写。在口语中，也常用“让”“叫”“给”来代替“被”。“让”“叫”后面的宾语不可以省略。例如：

When there is no need to emphasize the agent, the object can be omitted. In spoken language, “被” is often replaced by the prepositions “让”“叫” and “给”. When “让” or “叫” is used, the object cannot be omitted. E. g. ,

（1）我的书让他借走了。

（2）这件脏衣服叫妈妈洗得很干净。

（3）我的行李箱都给（安检员）打开了。

3. 能进入“被”字句的动词，比“把”字句动词范围稍大一些，“看见”“听见”等感觉类动词，“知道”“认为”等认知类动词，都可以进入“被”字句。例如：

Verbs that can be used in the “被” sentence are more than those of the “把” sentence. Sensory verbs such as “看见” and “听见” as well as cognitive verbs such as “知道” “认为” can all be used in the “被” sentence. E. g. ,

（1）他们说的话被坏人听见了。

（2）那件事被他知道了。

（3）早睡早起被大家认为是一个非常好的生活习惯。

4. 否定副词或能愿动词应在介词“被”“叫”“让”“给”前。否定句句尾不用“了”。例如：

The negative adverbs or modal verbs should be placed before “被” “叫” “让” “给”. “了” is not used at the end of the negative sentence. E. g. ,

（1）我们再不去买，那双鞋可能就被别人买走了。

（2）他低着头，不想被老师点名。

（3）我家前面的那棵大树还没被大风刮倒。

知识 2 Tip 2

“只有……才……”

“只有这样，才能抢到你想要的宝贝。”

“只有……才……”中，用“只有”提出特定条件，满足这个条件，就会产生“才”后面相应的结果。“只有”后面的这个条件是唯一的，不满足这个条件就不会产生这样的结果。例如：

In the structure “只有……才……”, “只有” is often used to put forward a specific condition, and if this condition is met, the corresponding results after “才” will be generated. The condition after “只有” is unique, and if this condition is not met, such a result will not occur. E. g. ,

(1) 只有会员才能看这个 App 上的视频。

(2) 同学们只有认真复习，才能通过考试。

(3) 奶奶常说，只有早睡早起，身体才会健康。

用法对比：“只有……才……”和“只要……就……”

Compare: “只有……才……” and “只要……就……”

“只有……才……”表示的是唯一条件、必需条件，即某一条件是唯一有用的，少了这一条件结果便不能产生，其他条件排除在外。“只要……就……”表示的是充分条件，即具备某一条件便可以产生某一结果，但可能还有别的条件可以产生相同的结果。例如：

“只有……才……” represents a unique and necessary condition, that is, a certain condition is the only useful, without which the result cannot be produced, and other conditions are excluded. “只要……就……” represents a sufficient condition, that is, a certain condition can produce a certain result, but there may be other conditions that can produce the same result. E. g. ,

只有……才……	只要……就……
只有会员才能看里面的视频。(只有一个办法：成为会员)	只要成为会员，就能看里面的视频。(成为会员是一种办法，但也可能有别的办法看到视频)
只有认真复习，才能通过考试。(只有一个办法：认真复习)	只要认真复习，就能通过考试。(认真复习是一种办法，但也可能有别的办法通过考试)
只有早睡早起，身体才会健康。(只有一个办法：早睡早起)	只要早睡早起，身体就会健康。(早睡早起是一种办法，但也可能有别的办法让身体健康)

知识3 Tip 3

"……是……，不过/但是……"

"经验丰富是丰富，不过也花了不少钱。"

"东西便宜是便宜，但是买来以后很多都用不着。"

"……是……，不过/但是……"常用来先肯定一个事实，之后用"不过""但是""就是"等进行转折，说出说话人最想表达的意思。例如：

"……是……，不过/但是……" is often used to concede a point first, and then "不过" "但是" "就是" is used to mtroduce what the speaker wants to express most. E. g. ,

(1) 这部手机好是好，不过价格稍微有点高。

(2) 这道菜好吃是好吃，但是做起来麻烦。

(3) 外卖方便是方便，就是容易让人变得越来越懒。

知识 4 Tip 4

“各”

“各家电商都会打折”

“各”指某个范围内的所有个体，用在名词或量词前。例如：

“各” refers to all individuals within a certain range. It is used before a noun or a measure word. E. g. ,

(1) 我的同学来自各个国家。

(2) 请各班班长去办公室拿书。

(3) 他是个“中国通”，中国各地的事情他都知道。

用法对比：“各”和“每”

Compare: “各” and “每”

1. “各”和“每”都指所有的个体，但意义上的着重点不同。“各”侧重同时遍指，“每”侧重于取出一个或一组为例子，强调个体的共同点。例如：

“各” and “每” both refer to all individuals, but the focus is different in meaning. “各” highlights individuality when an action applies to all members within a group, while “每” imparts a sense of uniformity and universality shared by all individuals. E. g. ,

（1）这家店一到晚上就打折，附近各小区的人都知道。

（2）我们各回各家，各找各妈。

（3）每个人都有一本中文书。

（4）他每半年就去医院做一次身体检查。

2. “各”可以直接加在一部分名词前，如地点、机构、组织等，“每”要跟量词或数量词一起才能加在名词前，只有数词“一”可以省去。例如：

“各” can be directly used in front of some nouns, such as place, institution, organization, etc. “每” can not stand immediately next to a noun unless it shows up together with a measure word or a numeral-classifier compound, only the numeral “一” can be omitted. E. g. ,

（1）各学校准备了一个节目。

每个学校准备了一个节目。

（2）她喜欢去各商店找便宜的东西。

她喜欢去每（一）家商店找便宜的东西。

（3）每两个小组之间进行一场比赛。（*各两个小组）

3. “各”后只能用一部分量词，如“个”“级”“位”“次”“类”“种”“样”“项”“条”“门”“路”“届”“方面”等，“每”后可以用各种量词。“各”不能和数量词结合，“每”可以和数量词结合。例如：

Certain quantifiers can be used after “各”, such as “个”“级”“位”“次”“类”“种”“样”“项”“条”“门”“路”“届”“方面”, etc. , but all kinds of quantifiers can be used after “每”. “各” cannot be combined with numeral-classifier compounds, but it works for “每”. E. g. ,

(1) 老师说我们各个都很棒。

(2) 各位先生里面请。

(3) 超市里摆着各种各样的水果。

(4) 我在中国的每一天都很开心。

(5) 这栋楼每两层就有一个休息室可以休息。

知识5 Tip 5

“着”

“买来以后很多都用不着”

动词“着”放在及物动词后表示达到目的。“动词＋着”后面可以带“了”“过”，中间可以加“得”“不”表示可能性，例如“用得着（有用）”“用不着（没用）”。例如：

The verb “着” is placed after a transitive verb to indicate the achievement of a goal. The “verb + 着” can be followed by “了” or “过”, and “得” or “不” can be added in the middle to indicate possibility, such as “用得着（useful)” or “用不着（unless)”. E. g. ,

(1) 箱子里是什么，你猜着了吗?

(2) 我个子不够高，拿不着，你帮我拿一下。

(3) 如果这个你用得着，我就送给你。

(4) 这些旧瓶子用不着，扔了吧。

练习 Exercises

1. 词语搭配。Complete the phrases.

________达人	继续________	举行________
浪费________	________经验	________包裹
________光	________仓库	________丰富

2. 选词填空。Choose the right words to fill in the blanks.

促销　堆　攻略　当天　仓库　秒杀　性价比　经验　浪费

（1）这么多包裹你要放在哪儿？我们的________早就满了。

（2）我的运气太好了，________到一条裤子，只要一块钱！

（3）这家店的东西________高，又好又便宜。

（4）旅行前，我喜欢上网看看别人写的旅游________。

（5）别________时间了，咱们快点儿开始吧。

（6）这件事还得问问班长，他比较有________。

（7）“双十一”的时候，很多网店都有________活动。

（8）深圳离广州挺近的，________就能回来。

（9）妹妹的房间________了很多书。

3. 按要求完成句子。Complete the sentences as required.

A. 用“光”“满”“上”“成”“着”填空。

（1）教室里坐________了人。

（2）外边太冷了，你还是把衣服穿________吧。

（3）他的房间特别乱，很多东西都找不__________。

（4）他饿坏了，才几分钟就把菜都给吃__________了。

（5）他昨天去银行，把人民币都换__________了美元。

B. 用“只要……就……”“只有……才……”改写句子。

（1）好好学习，可以找到好工作；会一门手艺，也可以找到好工作。

____

（2）好好学习，才能找到好工作；不好好学习，不能找到好工作。

____

（3）要是你去动物园玩儿，我就去；你不去，我一个人可能也会去。

____

（4）你去动物园玩儿，才能看到熊猫；不去动物园，看不到熊猫。

____

C. 用“不然”完成句子。

（1）要早睡早起，不然____________________________________。

（2）八点二十分了，快点儿走吧，不然______________________。

（3）出去玩儿的时候，要看好自己的钱包，不然______________。

（4）你最好把下周要做的事情写在本子上，不然______________。

（5）如果晚上 10 点还没回家，就给妈妈打个电话吧，不然_____。

D. 用“继续”“接着”填空。

（1）老板刚说了半个小时，经理__________又说了 20 分钟。

（2）上课了，同学们一个__________一个走进教室。

（3）我作业还没写完，我打算吃完饭__________写。

（4）老师说，小丽读完，小明__________读。

（5）我们休息一会儿吧，休息好了__________工作。

E. 用“每”“各”填空。

（1）我__________年都要出去旅游。

（2）请__________班同学快上车，我们马上就要出发了。

（3）__________一个认识他的人都喜欢他。

（4）他们俩__________想出来一个办法。

（5）__________十个同学里就有一个同学生病了。

（6）我记得他说的__________一句话。

4. 用“被”字句描述图片内容。 Describe the pictures with the “被” sentences.

（1）饭__________________

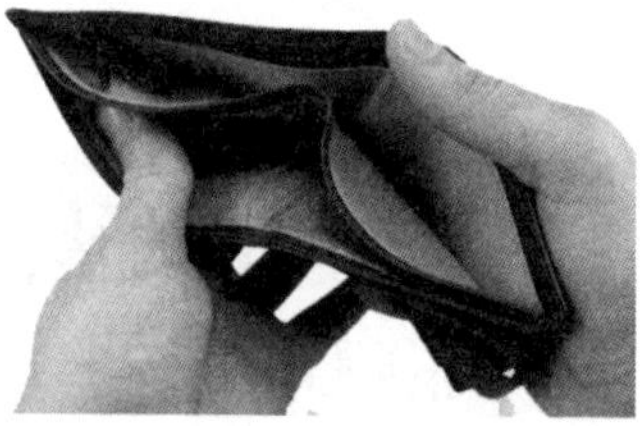

（2）钱__________________

（3）灯________________　　（4）衣服________________

（5）电视________________　　（6）小偷________________

5. 改错句。Correct the sentences.

（1）他散步光了。

____

（2）他看电影光了。

____

（3）我和朋友不约而同地在那家店见面。

____

（4）他们俩各不喜欢吃鱼。

____

（5）妹妹的房间到处都是一堆东西。

____

6. 根据课文完成句子。Complete the sentences according to the text.

（1）________________，我就去买。（如果）

（2）“双十一”的时候，我朋友设置了闹钟，________________________________。（一……就……）

（3）________________，才有可能抢到想买的东西。（只有）

（4）要提前做好攻略，________________。（不然）

（5）很多人________，不约而同地在“双十一”网购。（为了）

（6）那些快递公司的仓库，包裹堆得________。（像……一样）

（7）我朋友买了一台冰箱，________________。（比）

（8）“双十一”的东西________________，________________。（……是……，不过……）

7. 根据课文回答问题。Answer the questions according to the text.

课文 1

（1）阿里最近忙着干什么？为什么？

____

（2）“双十一”是什么？

____

（3）要想买到划算的东西，应该怎么做？

____

（4）“秒杀”是什么？怎么“秒杀”？

____

课文 2

（1）“双十一”的时候，快递公司的仓库常常是什么样子？为什么？

____

（2）为什么人们都在“双十一”这一天网购？

____

（3）今年“双十一”，“我”打算买东西吗？为什么？

____

8．我是网购达人。I am an online-shopping expert.

（1）速度与激情。

打开网购 App，找到网页上的秒杀活动，试一试，看哪位同学能抢到秒杀的商品。

（2）货比三家。

在几家网店比较同一种商品，说一说商品的价格、质量、服务、快递等方面有什么不同，写一写你的评价。

商品：________			
	网店 1	网店 2	网店 3
价格	☆ ☆ ☆ ☆ ☆	☆ ☆ ☆ ☆ ☆	☆ ☆ ☆ ☆ ☆
质量	☆ ☆ ☆ ☆ ☆	☆ ☆ ☆ ☆ ☆	☆ ☆ ☆ ☆ ☆
服务	☆ ☆ ☆ ☆ ☆	☆ ☆ ☆ ☆ ☆	☆ ☆ ☆ ☆ ☆
快递	☆ ☆ ☆ ☆ ☆	☆ ☆ ☆ ☆ ☆	☆ ☆ ☆ ☆ ☆

（3）辩论赛。

请以“便宜没好货，好货不便宜”为题进行辩论，写下双方不同的观点。

正方：便宜没好货。

反方：好货不便宜。

	正方：便宜没好货	反方：好货不便宜
观点		

9. 倒霉事大合集。A collection of bad luck.

（1）看电影或电视（如《人在囧途》《武状元苏乞儿》《唐伯虎点秋香》和卓别林的相关电影等），介绍里面人物最倒霉的一件事。（用上“被”字句，不少于100个字）

（2）每人说一件自己最倒霉的事，大家选出最倒霉的人，给他一个拥抱。（用上“被”字句，不少于100个字）

第九课　送货上门

Home delivery

课前热身 Warming up

你点过外卖吗？你觉得中国的外卖怎么样？

Have you ordered takeout? What do you think of Chinese takeout?

生词 New words

1	门铃	ménlíng	名	doorbell
2	响	xiǎng	动/形	to sound; to ring; noisy; loud
3	蔬菜	shūcài	名	vegetable

4	连…… 也……	lián…… yě……		even…
5	许多	xǔduō	数	many; much; a lot of
6	送货	sòng huò		to deliver goods
7	上门	shàngmén	动	to visit; to drop in
8	肉类	ròu lèi		meat
9	食品	shípǐn	名	food; foodstuff
10	登录	dēnglù	动	to log in
11	确定	quèdìng	形/动	to define; to fix; definite; certain
12	取件	qǔ jiàn		to collect a parcel; to pick-up
13	兴奋	xīngfèn	形	be excited; exciting
14	以内	yǐnèi	名	within
15	按摩师	ànmó shī		massagist
	按摩	ànmó	动	to massage
16	生鲜	shēng xiān		fresh food
17	立刻	lìkè	副	immediately
18	无论	wúlùn	连	no matter what, how, etc.
19	龙虾	lóngxiā	名	lobster
20	快捷	kuàijié	形	fast, speedy, rapid
21	现代	xiàndài	名/形	modern times; modern
22	高效	gāoxiào	形	efficient
23	未来	wèilái	名/形	future; coming; approaching

24	将	jiāng	副	will; be going to
25	不是…… 而是……	búshì…… érshì……		not…but…; however
26	智能化	zhìnéng huà		intelligent (used for machine, system, etc.)
27	无人	wú rén		unmanned; self-service
	无	wú	动	to not have; to be without
28	期待	qīdài	动	to expect; to await
29	从……来看	cóng……lái kàn		from the view of…
30	另一方面	lìng yì fāngmiàn		on the other hand
	方面	fāngmiàn	名	aspect; side
31	缺点	quēdiǎn	名	shortcoming; drawback
32	懒	lǎn	形	lazy
33	催	cuī	动	to urge; to hurry; to hasten

专名 Proper nouns

1	荷兰*	Hélán	the Netherlands
2	泰国*	Tàiguó	Thailand
3	澳大利亚*	Àodàlìyà	Australia
4	新西兰*	Xīnxīlán	New Zealand

课文 Text

课文1 Text 1

(门铃响了)

王乐乐：米亚，帮我开一下门，应该是我的快递来了。

…………

米　亚：哇，怎么都是蔬菜和水果？现在快递连这些也送吗？

王乐乐：对啊！现在网上买菜非常流行，附近许多超市都能送货上门。不只是蔬菜水果，肉类、海鲜等食品也都可以送。

米　亚：服务真不错！看着还挺新鲜的。

王乐乐：那当然，我下单才半个多小时就到了。

米　亚：啊，这么快！快教教我，怎么买的？

王乐乐：和淘宝差不多，下载他们的 App，用手机登录，选择自己想买的东西，然后确定取件的时间，最后付钱就可以了。

米　亚：没想到这么方便。看你买了这么多菜，我口水都要流下来了！好久没尝到你的手艺了。

王乐乐：哈哈，一看到吃的你就兴奋。好，我马上去做。

课文2 Text 2

累的时候怎么办？打个电话，一个小时以内就能叫按摩师上门服务。想吃生鲜怎么办？上网预订一下，新鲜又好吃的美味立刻送到家门口。

无论是荷兰的鲜花，还是泰国的榴莲；无论是澳大利亚的龙虾，还是新西兰的牛奶……只需要一部手机，你就能把它们叫到家里来，连家门都不用出。方便快捷的快递服务让现代人的生活变得那么简单又高效。也许在不远的未来，把快递包裹送上门的将不是快递小哥，而是智能化的无人机和无人车。亲爱的你，期待吗？

不过，从另一方面来看，上门服务也有一个缺点，那就是让现代人变得越来越懒，耐心变得越来越差。说到这儿，我的外卖怎么还没有来？都半个小时了，我得打电话催一催了……

语言知识 Language guidelines

知识1 Tip 1

“连……也/都……”

“现在快递连这些也送吗？”“连家门都不用出”

介词“连”后一般是名词，也可以是动词、小句、数量短语，数量短语中的数词限于“一”；“连……”后面常用“也”“都”等，“连”前面还可以加“甚至”。在肯定句中，多用“连……都……”；在否定句中，“连……都……”“连……也……”都可以用。“连……也/都……”表示在陈述中，相比较而言说话人认为不太可能的对象都发生了某种情况，言外之意是其他对象就更是这样了，这是少见的情况。例如：

The preposition “连” is usually followed by a noun, but it can also precede a verb, a clause, or a quantitative phrase. The numeral in the quantitative phrase is limited to “一” in this case. “也” “都” and so on can be used after “连……”, and “甚至” can also added in front of

“连”. In a positive sentence, “连……都……” is used more often; while in a negative sentence, both “连……都……” and “连……也……” can be used. “连……也/都……” is used in a statement that something has happened to the objects that the speaker considers unlikely, and the implication is that other objects are even more so, this is a rare occurrence. E. g. ,

(1) 这道题太简单，连小孩子都知道。

(2) 这个小偷太穷了，偷钱，偷衣服，偷面包，甚至连旧报纸都偷。

(3) 她难过极了，看见最喜欢的蛋糕，连尝也不想尝。

(4) 我最近太忙了，连一天也没休息。

(5) 我连他叫什么名字都不知道，更不要说了解他了。

知识❷ Tip 2

“许多”

“附近许多超市都能送货上门。”

1. 数词“许多”表示数量多，多用于书面语。例如：

The numeral “许多” indicates a large quantity and is often used in written language. E. g. ,

(1) 地铁上有许多人。

(2) 这个地方，我去了许多次。

(3) 这本书上的许多字我都不认得。

2. “动词/形容词＋许多”表示程度或数量变化较大，形容词多为单音节，动词和形容词后面常加“了”。例如：

“动词/形容词＋许多” indicates a great change in degree or quantity. The adjectives are mostly monosyllabic, and verbs and adjectives are often followed by “了”. E. g. ,

（1）他出国留学了5年，回来以后性格改变了许多。

（2）这件衣服大了许多，我穿不合适。

（3）这学期我交了两个中国朋友，每天用中文聊天，我的中文流利了许多。

用法对比：“许多”和“很多”

Compare: “许多” and “很多”

1. “许多”前可以用指示词“这”“那”“这么”“那么”，“很多”不能。例如：

“许多” can be preceded by demonstrative words “这”“那”“这么” and “那么”, but “很多” cannot. E. g. ,

（1）你做了这么许多菜，我们俩怎么吃得完？（*很多）

（2）现在管不了这许多了，先把她送到医院吧。（*很多）

（3）他真厉害，一下子说了那许多中国的地名。（*很多）

2. “许多”的重叠形式有“许多许多”和“许许多多”两种，都强调数量多，用法和名词一样，也可以修饰名词，而“很多”的重叠式只有“很多很多”。例如：

There are two reduplicated forms of “许多”, namely “许多许多” and “许许多多”. Both emphasizing a large quantity, the two phrases can function as nouns and modify nouns, while the only one reduplicated form of “很多” is “很多很多”. E. g. ,

(1) 这种电影我看过许许多多。(很多很多)
(2) 我来这儿已经有许多许多年了。(很多很多)
(3) 许许多多的人都来看这场比赛。(很多很多)

知识3 Tip 3

“立刻”

“美味立刻送到家门口”

副词“立刻”表示紧接着某个时候，马上。后面可以加动词，也可以是表示状态变化的形容词。例如：

The adverb “立刻” means “immediately” or “right away”. It can be followed by a verb or an adjective indicating a change of state. E. g. ,

(1) 老师不说话了，教室里立刻安静下来。
(2) 老板让我立刻去他的办公室。
(3) 电话响了，他立刻跑去接电话。

用法对比：“立刻”和“马上”

Compare: “立刻” and “马上”

“立刻”表示事情发生的时间比较紧迫，而“马上”表示的紧迫性有时幅度较大，不一定真的很快发生。例如：

“立刻” signifies that the time when something happens is relatively constrained, while “马上” carries a slightly more relaxing tone and something may not necessarily happen without any delay. E. g. ,

（1）看到他快要摔倒了，我马上跑了过去，把他扶稳。（立刻）

（2）马上就考试了，你怎么还没复习？（＊立刻）

（3）冬天快结束了，马上就春天了。（＊立刻）

知识4 Tip 4

“无论……，都/也……”

“无论是荷兰的鲜花，还是泰国的榴莲；无论是澳大利亚的龙虾，还是新西兰的牛奶……只需要一部手机，你就能把它们叫到家里来。”

连词“无论”表示在任何条件下结果或结论都不会改变，后面常加表示任指的疑问代词，或表示选择关系的并列成分，后边常有“都”或“也”呼应。例如：

The conjunction “无论” indicates that the result or conclusion will not change under any conditions. It is often followed by interrogative pronouns indicating indefinite reference, or the paratactic components indicating selection. Usually, there is “都” or “也” behind it. E. g. ,

（1）无论晴天还是下雨，他都没有迟到过。

（2）大家无论有什么困难，都喜欢去找班长。

（3）这件事无论对你还是对我都很重要。

（4）无论这个工作多么难，我们也要把它做好。

用法对比："无论"和"不管"

Compare："无论" and "不管"

"无论"和"不管"都是连词。用于前一小句，表示任指各种条件；后一小句常有"都""总""全""就""也"等词语与前句呼应，表示结果不变，两个词常可以通用。

Both "无论" and "不管" are conjunctions. They are used in the preceding clause to indicate any conditions. In the latter clause, words such as "都", "总", "全", "就" and "也" are often used in response to the preceding clause, indicating that the result remains the same. The two words can often be used interchangeably.

两个词的区别：

The difference between the two words：

1. 连词"无论"多用于书面语，连词"不管"多用于口语。因此，"无论"后面能用"如何""是否""与否"等书面词语，"不管"不可以。例如：

The conjunction "无论" is more often used in written language, while the conjunction "不管" is often used in spoken language. Therefore, "无论" can be followed by "如何" "是否" "与否" and other written words, while "不管" cannot. E. g. ,

不管	无论
不管怎么样，我都会把工作完成。	无论如何，我都会把工作完成。
不管顺不顺路，我们都要去一趟。	无论顺路与否，我们都要去一趟。

2. 此外，“不管”后面可以用“名词+不+名词”，“无论”一般没有这种用法。例如：

In addition, “不管” can be followed by “noun + 不 + noun”, while “无论” generally can not be used like this. E. g.,

（1）A：这份工作钱不多，你要干吗？

B：我不管钱不钱，有工作就行了。

（2）A：现在下大雨，别去了吧。

B：不管大雨不大雨，我是一定要去的。

知识5 Tip 5

“不是……而是……”

“不是快递小哥，而是智能化的无人机和无人车。”

“不是……而是……”用于并列复句，否定“不是”之后的情况，肯定“而是”之后的情况。例如：

“不是……而是……” is used in a compound sentence to negate the situation after “不是” and affirm the situation after “而是”. E. g.,

（1）他不是我的哥哥而是我的弟弟。

（2）这道菜不是我做的，而是他做的。

（3）生病了，他不是去医院看医生，而是自己去药店买药。

（4）这件事，我不是不知道，而是不想告诉你，怕你担心。

练习 Exercises

1. 词语消消乐。 Play the words game.

~~水果~~	流行	手机	送货
食品	上门	~~蔬菜~~	购物
非常	到家	时间	登录
网上	收货	服务	生鲜

例如：蔬菜水果*

________________　________________　________________

________________　________________　________________

________________　________________　________________

________________　________________　________________

________________　________________　________________

________________　________________　________________

________________　________________　________________

________________　________________　________________

* 搭配的词语意思合理即可，所给的词语可重复使用。

2. 选词填空。Choose the right words to fill in the blanks.

上门　登录　立刻　选择　高效　下载　懒　催　确定

(1) 都十分钟了他怎么还没来，你打电话__________一下他。

(2) 我经常在手机上__________电影看。

(3) 你要在网上购物的话先要__________购物网站。

(4) 现在生鲜食品也可以送货__________了。

(5) 你怎么这么__________，脏衣服都一个星期没洗了。

(6) 明天有考试？你__________吗？

(7) 听到门铃响，他__________去开门。

(8) 我__________来中国学习中文是因为我喜欢中国文化。

(9) 我爸爸做事很__________，一会儿就把事情都做好了。

3. 用下面的词语改写句子。Rewrite the sentences with the given words.

A. 连……也……

(1) 大人认识这个字。小朋友认识这个字。

____

(2) 他不会说中文。他不会用中文说“你好”。

____

(3) 很多人不相信他说的话。他的爸爸妈妈不相信他说的话。

____

B. 无论……还是……

(1) 老师喜欢他。同学喜欢他。

____

（2）她中文说得很流利。她英文说得很流利。

____

（3）他学习很好。他运动很好。

____

C. 不是……而是……

（1）这本书我在网上买的。这本书我不是去书店买的。

____

（2）他来中国看朋友。他不是来中国旅游。

____

（3）他周末去踢球。他周末不去图书馆看书。

____

4. 改错句。Correct the sentences.

（1）我去超市买生鲜的鱼。

____

（2）不好意思，我不在宿舍，可以明天取件快递吗？

____

（3）今天下午快递小哥送货我的东西。

____

（4）当我回国时，我一定上门你的家。

____

（5）我以内三年就可以毕业了。

____

(6) 这道题很难，连老师不会做这个题。

____

(7) 我妈妈说我是最智能化的孩子。

____

(8) 我不是中国人，而是我看起来像中国人。

____

(9) 他被警察罚款五百元，因为开车开得太快捷了。

____

(10) 这种药对身体很高效。

____

5. 组句。 Rearrange the words to form a sentence.

(1) 我 你 一下 帮 开 麻烦 门

____

(2) 流行 买菜 现在 非常 网上

____

(3) 就 我 才 小时 到了 下单 半个多

____

(4) 越来越 现代人 服务 让 上门 懒 变得

____

(5) 高效 人们 快递 让 的 变得 生活

____

6. 完成句子。 Complete the sentences.

(1) 这道菜太咸了，______________________。（连……也……）

（2）周末的时候，________________________________。（许多）

（3）托运的行李________________________________。（以内）

（4）听到下课铃响了，____________________________。（立刻）

（5）________________________，她都是很开心的样子。（无论）

（6）学校的毕业晚会________________________________。（将）

（7）上课的时候，他__________________。（不是……而是……）

（8）________________，这部手机的性价比很高。（从……来看）

（9）__________________，“双十一”买很划算。（从……来看）

（10）这台照相机一方面价格高，________________________，还是别买了。（另一方面）

7. **根据课文回答问题**。Answer the questions according to the text.

课文 1

（1）门铃响了，是谁来了？

____

（2）快递小哥送的是什么？

____

（3）怎么在网上买菜？

____

课文 2

（1）现代人的生活怎么样？为什么？

____

（2）以后人们的生活还会有什么变化？

（3）你想回到以前没有快递服务的生活吗？为什么？

8. 购物比赛。A shopping competition.

（1）打开任意一个生鲜食品的购物 App，挑选 6 个或 6 个以上的商品放到购物车，使商品的总价格刚好为 100 元，最快完成的同学获胜。

（2）你什么时候会去超市、市场买生鲜食品？什么时候会上网买生鲜食品？比一比两种方式的优点和缺点。

方式	优点	缺点
去超市、市场买生鲜食品		
上网买生鲜食品		

（3）哎呀，奶奶！

你的奶奶很不喜欢用手机，觉得手机不方便，过着很传统的生活。一天天气不太好，奶奶的腿也有点儿疼，但是为了给家人做饭，一大早又带上钱包、小推车出去买菜了……你看到奶奶的样子很心疼，于是决定教会奶奶用手机……

根据上面的情景组织对话，表演出来。练习对话时，尽可能多地使用下面的词语和句式。

参考词语	送货上门、许多、肉类、食品、生鲜、登录、确定、取件、以内、立刻、快捷、现代、高效、未来、无人、智能化、缺点、差、催……
参考句式	连……也…… 无论……，也/都…… 不是……而是…… 一方面……，另一方面…… 从……来看

9．小练笔。Writing.

如果你出生在 100 年以后，你的生活将会是什么样子？（不少于 100 个字）

第十课　减肥

Lose weight

课前热身 Warming up

你想减肥吗？你知道有哪些减肥方法吗？

Do you want to lose weight? Do you know any way to lose weight?

生词 New words

1	终于	zhōngyú	副	finally
2	饼干	bǐnggān	名	biscuit
3	体重	tǐzhòng	名	weight
4	节食	jiéshí	动	to be on a diet
5	减肥	jiǎnféi	动	to lose weight

6	胖	pàng	形	fat
7	必要	bìyào	形	necessary
8	饮食	yǐnshí	名	diet; eating and drinking
9	均衡*	jūnhéng	形	balanced
10	身材	shēncái	名	figure
11	随便	suíbiàn	动/形	to do as one pleases; casual; careless
12	相信	xiāngxìn	动	to believe in
13	假	jiǎ	形	false; fake; artificial
14	吃货	chīhuò	名	foodie
15	宅女	zháinǚ	名	homebody
16	减	jiǎn	动	to decrease; to subtract
17	保持	bǎochí	动	to maintain; to hold; to keep
18	至少	zhìshǎo	副	at least
19	升温	shēngwēn	动	to warm up
20	夏装	xiàzhuāng	名	summer wear
21	竟然	jìngrán	副	unexpectedly; to one's surprise
22	天呐*	tiān na		oh my God
23	管	guǎn	动	to supervise; to control; to discipline (children or students)
24	嘴	zuǐ	名	mouth

25	迈	mài	动	to step; to stride
26	腿	tuǐ	名	leg
27	控制	kòngzhì	动	to control
28	热量	rèliàng	名	calorie; heat
29	戒	jiè	动	to give up; to stop
30	甜食	tiánshí	名	dessert
31	代替	dàitì	动	to replace
32	主食	zhǔshí	名	staple food
33	有氧运动	yǒuyǎng yùndòng		aerobic exercise
34	勤	qín	形	often; frequent; diligent
35	效果	xiàoguǒ	名	effect
36	恐怕	kǒngpà	副	to be afraid that…; maybe
37	副作用	fùzuòyòng	名	side effect
38	唉*	ài	叹	(sigh of sadness or regret) oh; ah; well

课文 Text

课文1 Text 1

（下课铃响了）

艾文：终于下课了，我快饿死了！

安娜：想起来了，我带了饼干和巧克力，你要不要？

艾文：当然……哇，味道不错。

安娜：米亚，你要吗？

米亚：看起来很好吃！可是最近我的体重又增加了，我要节食减肥。

艾文：你又不胖，没必要减肥吧！

安娜：是啊，再说，我觉得节食对身体不好。

米亚：可是吃零食容易胖啊！我决定把零食收起来，只吃点儿水果和蔬菜。

安娜：饮食最好要均衡，只吃水果、蔬菜也不一定好。其实只要多运动，吃点儿零食也没关系。

米亚：你身材这么好，当然可以随便吃。

安娜：也许你们不相信，我以前比现在重10多斤！

艾文：真的假的？我想不出来你胖的样子。

安娜：我以前是个吃货，还是个宅女，每天除了吃就是睡，衣服都大了一码！

米亚：那你是怎么减下来的？

安娜：很简单，保持饮食均衡，多运动，我每周至少去三次健身房呢。

课文2 Text 2

今天升温了，我准备穿去年才买的夏装去上课，没想到以前能穿上的裤子现在竟然穿不下了——天呐，我又胖了！该减肥了！说到减肥，人们最常说的一句话就是“管住嘴，迈开腿”。

“管住嘴”就是节食减肥，要控制饮食，少吃高热量的食品，戒奶茶、戒甜食、戒炸鸡……用蔬菜和水果代替主食。可是我想起来，朋友告诉我，只靠节食减肥对身体也不好，还要多运动。“迈开腿”就是运动减肥，多做有氧运动，比如跑步、游泳、骑车，勤锻炼身体。但是，运动需要长时间坚持才有效果，我比较懒，肯定不能坚持下去。

还有一个办法，就是喝减肥茶，吃减肥药。不过，这些恐怕对身体有副作用。唉，减肥真是太不容易了！

语言知识 Language guidelines

知识1 Tip 1

“终于”

“终于下课了，我快饿死了！”

“终于”表示经过较长过程，最后出现了某种情况，多用于希望达到的结果。例如：

“终于” means that something happens at the end of a long process. It is mainly used to describe desired results. E. g. ,

(1) 我终于拿到了 HSK 4 级证书。

(2) 我等你半天，你终于来了。

(3) 他每天坚持锻炼，身体终于好起来了。

用法对比：“终于”和“到底”

Compare：“终于” and “到底”

“终于”和“到底”都是副词，表示“到尽头，最终”，可以通用。例如：

“终于” and “到底” are both adverbs, with the meaning of “to the end, finally”. They are interchangeable. E. g. ,

(1) 我终于学会骑自行车了。(到底)

(2) 这本书我终于看完了。(到底)

(3) 问题终于解决了。(到底)

两个词的区别：

The difference between the two words:

1. 副词“到底”多用于口语，一般说成“到底……了”。例如：

The adverb “到底” is often used in spoken Chinese and is usually used in the structure “到底……了”. E. g. ,

(1) 他想了半天，后来到底决定去了。

(2) 你到底回来了，我还以为今天你不回来呢。

(3) 她看起来不开心，于是我说了许多笑话，到底把她弄笑了。

副词“终于”一般用于书面语，可以说成“终于……了”，也可以不带“了”。例如：

The adverb “终于” is generally used in writing. “终于……了” is a handy phrase, and “了” can be omitted. E. g. ,

(1) 辛苦了 20 年，他终于取得了成功。

(2) 这个国家终于赢得了自由。

(3) 这件事发生后的一年，他终于离开家，和几个朋友去北京开始新的生活。

2. 此外，副词“到底”可以用在问句里，表示深究。“终于”没有这种用法。例如：

In addition, the adverb “到底” can be used in questions to indicate a thorough investigation. There is no such usage of “终于”. E. g. ,

(1) 一会儿说去，一会儿说不去，你到底去不去?

(2) 我说了这么多遍，你到底明白了没有?

(3) 你到底怎么了？为什么要哭?

3. 副词“到底”还有“毕竟”的意思，“终于”没有。例如：

The adverb “到底” also means “after all”, but “终于” does not. E. g. ,

(1) 到底你是她妈妈，她听你的，不听我的。

(2) 到底是南方比北方暖和，现在北方都下雪了，南方才穿件薄外套。

(3) 他们到底年轻，爬了这么久都不觉得累。

知识2 Tip 2

“又 + 不/没”

“你又不胖，没必要减肥吧！”

副词“又”用在否定句中，用来加强否定语气，表示作为下文所指的理由，“又”要轻读。例如：

The adverb “又” is used in a negative sentence to strengthen the negative mood, leading to the reason given below. “又” should be read in a neutral tone. E. g. ,

(1) 你又不胖，没必要减肥。

(2) 他怎么知道的？我又没告诉他。

(3) 你又不是没长手，不会自己拿吗？

知识3 Tip 3

“再说”

“你又不胖，没必要减肥吧！再说，我觉得节食对身体不好。”

“再说”常用在口语中，表示进一步说明理由或进行补充，常用在后一个理由前。例如：

“再说” is often used in spoken Chinese to give further explanation or supplement, as the conjunction introducing the last reason. E. g. ,

(1) 这件衣服不好看，再说，价格也不便宜，别买了。

(2) 外面阳光好，我们出去逛逛吧！再说，你一个人在家多无聊啊！

(3) 你不用谢我，我们是朋友，再说，这是我应该做的。

注意：“再说”和“再＋说”意思不同。“再＋说”的意思是：重复说或者某件事现在不适合做或不想做，等以后有机会再做。例如：

Note: “再说” and “再＋说” have different meanings. “再＋说”

means “to repeat” or denotes that someting will get done in the future since there is no right timing now. E. g. ,

(1) 不好意思，刚才我没听清楚，你能再说一遍吗?

(2) 哎呀，这件事你都说了十遍了，别再说了。

(3) 今天我很忙，这件事明天再说。

(4) 这个东西你先拿去用，什么时候还我，过几天再说。

知识4 Tip 4

趋向补语的引申用法

趋向动词大多有引申意义，常表示动作的结果。常见的趋向动词有“上”“下”“起来”“出来”“下来”“下去”等。

Most directional verbs have extended meanings to indicate the result of the action. Common directional verbs include “上”“下”“起来”“出来”“下来”“下去”, etc.

“上”

“以前能穿上的裤子现在竟然穿不下了”

1. “动词 + 上 + 名词”，表示动作有结果，有时有合拢的意思。例如：

“Verb + 上 + noun” indicates that an action has produced a result, sometimes suggesting the state of closing. E. g. ,

(1) 你最后走的话，别忘了把教室的窗户关上，门锁上。

(2) 外面太亮了，把窗帘拉上吧!

（3）先盖上盖子，再把饭菜放到微波炉里加热。

2.“动词 + 上 + 名词”，有时也表示达到一定的目的。例如：

“Verb + 上 + noun” sometimes also indicates the achievement of a goal. E. g. ,

（1）她努力了一年，终于选上了优秀学生。

（2）认真工作了五年，他不仅当上了经理，还买上了汽车，住上了新房。

（3）我弟弟考上了自己喜欢的大学，我们全家人都很开心。

“下”

“以前能穿上的裤子现在竟然穿不下了”

“动词 + 得/不 + 下（ + 数量 + 名词）”，有时表示空间能不能容纳一定的数量。动词多为“坐”“站”“睡”“躺”“停”“装”“容”“盛”“放”“住”等。例如：

“Verb + 得/不 + 下（ + numeral + noun）” sometimes indicates the ability of a space to accommodate a certain amount of people or things. The verbs used in this structure include “坐”“站”“睡”“躺”“停”“装”“容”“盛”“放”“住” and so on. E. g. ,

（1）这辆大巴够大，我们十几个人坐得下，没问题。

（2）我东西特别多，这个小行李箱放不下。

（3）我们一家五口人，50 平方米的房子肯定住不下。

“起来”

“我决定把零食收起来”

1. “动词+起来”，表示将事物放在一起，或使东西从分散到集中。例如：

“Verb + 起来” means putting things together or bringing things together. E. g.,

(1) 这根绳子断了，你能把它们接起来吗？

(2) 这道题是让你把拼音和词语连起来。

(3) 马上考试了，大家把书、手机都收起来吧！

(4) 妈妈把爸爸的旧报纸都捆起来了，准备卖掉。

2. “动词+起来”，还表示动作开始并继续进行。动词和“起来”中间一般不能加“得”“不”。例如：

“Verb + 起来” also indicates the beginning and continuation of an action. “得” or “不” can't be added between the verb and “起来”. E. g.,

(1) 看到他的照片，大家都笑起来了。

(2) 枪声一响，运动员们跑了起来。

(3) 你怎么哭起来了？到底发生了什么事？

注意：如果是“离合词+起来”，常需要将离合词、“起来”分开，写成“动词+起+宾语+来”。例如：

Note: In “detachable word + 起来”, it is often necessary to separate them and have it written as "verb + 起 + object + 来". E. g. ,

(1) 刚才天气还不错，怎么突然下起雨来了？

(2) 他们俩坐在一起，上课没几分钟就说起话来了。

(3) 主人和客人们都特别开心，大家唱起歌、跳起舞来。

3. "形容词 + 起来"，表示一种状态开始并发展，程度在继续加深，形容词多为积极的意义。例如：

"Adjective + 起来" implies the start and development of a state, with the degree increasing as time goes by. The adjectives are mostly positive. E. g. ,

(1) 吃了药以后，我的身体一天天好起来了。

(2) 春天到了，天气慢慢暖和起来。

(3) 真羡慕她，每天吃那么多也胖不起来。

4. 此外，"想起来"常表示记忆的恢复。例如：

In addition, "想起来" often indicates the recovery of memory. E. g. ,

(1) 我想起来了，我有饼干和巧克力。

(2) 你把我的钥匙放哪儿了？你想起来了没有？

(3) 很多小学同学的名字，我已经想不起来了。

“出来”

“我想不出来你胖的样子。”

1. “动词+出来（+名词）”，表示人或事物随着动作由隐蔽到显露。例如：

“Verb + 出来（+ noun）” means that a person or thing goes from concealment to revelation with action taking place. E. g. ,

（1）这两幅图有什么不同，你看出来了吗？

（2）盒子里是什么礼物，你猜得出来猜不出来？

（3）这一束花和这几句话把他对你的爱全都表达出来了。

2. “动词+出来（+名词）”，表示动作完成，兼有使一种新事物产生或从无到有的意思，名词常放在“出”和“来”之间。例如：

“Verb + 出来（+ noun）” indicates the completion of an action and also has the meaning of causing a new thing to emerge or develop from nothing. The noun is often placed between “出” and “来”. E. g. ,

（1）老师要求的那篇文章我终于写出来了。

（2）老板，我们要的20套衣服，这星期能做出来吗？

（3）我最近很忙，抽不出时间来运动。

因此，“想出来”表示产生新的想法，与“想起来”意思不同。例如：

Therefore, “想出来” means generating a new idea, which is different from “想起来”. E. g. ,

想出来	想起来
他临时想出来一个办法。（新办法）	他想起来以前在书上看到过这个办法。（以前看过的）
他想出来一个好玩的游戏。（新游戏）	我想起来我玩过这个游戏。（以前玩过的）
这个“汉字”是我想出来的，字典里没有。（新“汉字”）	我突然想起来这个汉字怎么写了。（以前学过的）

“下来”

“那你是怎么减下来的？”

1. “动词 + 下来”，表示通过动作使事物固定在一定的位置上。例如：

“Verb + 下来” indicates fixing something in a certain position through action. E. g. ,

（1）红灯亮了，路上的车都停了下来。

（2）刚才黑板上的句子你写下来了吗？

（3）这儿的风景真美，我要把它拍下来。

（4）我们几个打算周末出去玩儿，你呢？你的时间定得下来定不下来？

2. “动词 + 下来”，表示动作从过去继续到现在。例如：

“Verb + 下来” indicates that the action continues from the past to the present. E. g. ,

（1）3000 米虽然很长，但是他跑下来了，还得了第一名。

（2）这篇课文又长又难，不过我最后读下来了，意思也明白了。

（3）运动减肥是很不错的方法，可是我没有坚持下来。

3. “形容词 + 下来”，表示某种状态开始并继续发展，强调状态的开始出现。例如：

“Adjective + 下来” indicates the coming and continued development of a certain state. It emphasizes the beginning of a state. E. g. ,

（1）晚上 6 点，外面就暗下来了。

（2）一下课教室外面就热闹起来，但是上课后很快就安静下来。

（3）刚才他十分激动，现在终于平静下来了。

“下去”

“我比较懒，肯定不能坚持下去。”

1. “动词 + 下去”，表示正在进行的动作仍然继续进行。例如：

“Verb + 下去” indicates the action in progress will continue. E. g. ,

（1）虽然我回国了，但是中文我还会学下去。

（2）老板讲了一个小时了，再讲下去大家都要睡着了。

（3）这部电影真没意思，我看不下去了，换个电影看看吧！

2. “形容词 + 下去”，表示某种状态已经存在并将继续发展，强调继续发展。形容词多用表示消极意义的。例如：

“Adjective + 下去” indicates that a certain state has already existed and will continue to develop. It emphasizes continued development. The adjectives used in this structure often connote negativity. E. g. ,

(1) 你都180斤了，少吃一点儿吧，不能再胖下去了。

(2) 天呐，热死我了，手机上说可能还会热下去。

(3) 适当放松可以，要是一直放松下去，恐怕以后工作都丢了。

知识 5 Tip 5

教学视频

“竟然”

“没想到以前能穿上的裤子现在竟然穿不下了”

副词“竟然”表示出乎意料、没想到，有时也单说“竟”。后面可以加动词，也可以加形容词。例如：

The adverb “竟然” means “unexpectedly”, and sometimes it is abbreviated as “竟”. It can stand before a verb or an adjective after it. E. g. ,

(1) 他太忙了，竟然忘记了吃饭。

(2) 我找了半天，手机竟然在这儿。

(3) 没想到这次的考试竟然这么简单。

(4) 你没想到吧，他竟是第一个来的人。

用法对比：“竟然”和“没想到”

Compare: “竟然” and “没想到”

“竟然”和“没想到”表示的意思相同。不同的是，“竟然”是副词，不能单独作谓语，“没想到”可以。“没想到”和“竟然”可以用在同一个句子中。例如：

“竟然” means the same as “没想到”, but as an adverb, it can not be used as a predicate, while “没想到” can; “竟然” and “没想到” can be used in the same sentence. E. g. ,

（1）你竟然是第一个来的人。

你是第一个来的人，我没想到。/我没想到你是第一个来的人。

我没想到你竟然是第一个来的人。

（2）他竟然当了班长。

你没想到吧，他竟然当了班长。

我们都没想到竟然选他当班长。

练习 Exercises

1. **看图片写词语。** Write the words according to the pictures.

（1）________

（2）________

（3）________

（4）____________

（5）____________

（6）____________

（7）____________

（8）____________

（9）____________

（10）____________

（11）____________

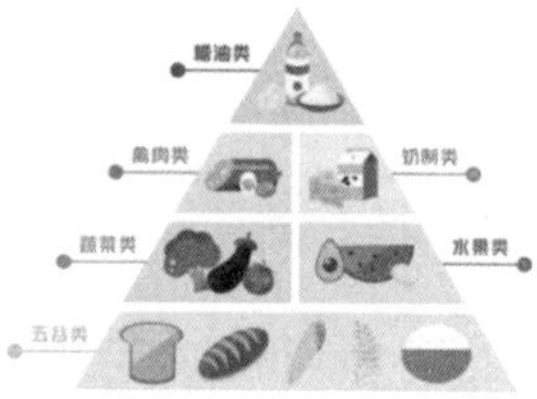

（12）____________

2．词语搭配。Complete the phrases.

戒__________	增加__________	控制__________
相信__________	__________体重	__________身材
__________均衡	代替__________	保持__________

3．选词填空。 Choose the right words to fill in the blanks.

均衡　随便　必要　简单　终于　保持　增加　至少　控制

（1）想减肥成功，每次＿＿＿＿＿锻炼 30 分钟。
（2）火车开了 20 个小时，＿＿＿＿＿到了这个地方。
（3）大家都明白了，我就没有＿＿＿＿＿再说一遍了。
（4）你吃这么多又不常锻炼，体重只会＿＿＿＿＿。
（5）健康＿＿＿＿＿的饮食可以让你越来越年轻。
（6）今晚的晚会很重要，你的衣服不能穿得很＿＿＿＿＿。
（7）这次考试题目特别＿＿＿＿＿，一半的同学都拿到了满分。
（8）生气的时候，我觉得我不能＿＿＿＿＿我自己。
（9）在图书馆看书不能大声说话，要＿＿＿＿＿安静。

4．选词填空。 Choose the right words to fill in the blanks.

起来　出来　下来　下去

（1）这个人我认识，但是一下子想不＿＿＿＿＿叫什么了。
（2）听到他说错了，同学们都笑＿＿＿＿＿了。
（3）中文很重要，回国以后我还要继续学＿＿＿＿＿。
（4）今天的作业是什么，我一下子想不＿＿＿＿＿了。
（5）夏天到了，天气会一直热＿＿＿＿＿。
（6）跑 3000 米虽然很累，但是你坚持＿＿＿＿＿了，真了不起。
（7）我喝＿＿＿＿＿了，这是红茶。
（8）你把我的电话号码记＿＿＿＿＿吧。
（9）你听得＿＿＿＿＿这是谁唱的歌吗？

（10）这两张图有什么不一样，你看__________了吗？

（11）啊，我想__________了，你是我三年前的同学。

（12）我工作比较忙，一个小时也抽不__________。

5．改错句。Correct the sentences.

（1）他的身体均衡。

____

（2）教室的温度升温了。

____

（3）服务员，这个碗有点儿脏，请问能代替吗？

____

（4）我把这件衣服代替那件脏衣服。

____

（5）下个月我学习中文下去。

____

（6）我明年打算住在中国下去。

____

（7）我以为他是中国人，竟然他是法国人。

____

（8）他不勤生气，每天都很开心。

____

6．根据课文完成句子。Complete the sentences according to the text.

（1）我朋友想减肥，但是她看起来不胖，____________________

____。（必要）

（2）但是，我的体重增加了，以前的衣服____。（竟然）

（3）________________________，就要少吃多运动。（说到）

（4）减肥时不能________________________________。（随便）

（5）应该把________________________________。（戒）

（6）运动需要长时间坚持，____健身房。（至少）

（7）可是我比较懒，____。（动词＋下去）

（8）吃减肥药减肥________________________________。（恐怕）

7. 根据课文回答问题。Answer the questions according to the text.

课文 1

（1）米亚为什么不要饼干和巧克力？

____

（2）安娜觉得米亚的想法对吗？为什么？

____

（3）安娜以前的身材怎么样？她是怎么减肥的？

____

课文 2

（1）“我”怎么知道该减肥了？

____

（2）“管住嘴，迈开腿”是什么意思？具体应该怎么做？

____

（3）“我”觉得减肥容易吗？为什么？

____

8. 我是减肥专家。I am the expert of weight loss.

（1）听中文歌《卡路里》，学习其中和减肥有关系的词语。

歌词选段：

拜拜　甜甜圈　珍珠奶茶方便面/火锅米饭大盘鸡　拿走拿走别客气

拜拜　咖啡因　戒掉可乐戒油腻/沙发外卖玩游戏　别再熬夜伤身体

来来　后转体　高温瑜伽仰卧起/动感单车普拉提　保温杯里泡枸杞

来来　深呼吸　晨跑夜跑游几米/平板哑铃划船机　不达目的不放弃

 tiántiánquān 甜甜圈 doughnut	 zhēnzhū nǎichá 珍珠奶茶 bubble milk tea	 fāngbiànmiàn 方便面 instant noodles
 huǒguō 火锅 hotpot	 dàpánjī 大盘鸡 saute spicy chicken	 kāfēiyīn 咖啡因 caffeine

 áo yè 熬夜 stay up late	 zhuǎntǐ 转体 twist	 yújiā 瑜伽 yoga
 yǎngwòqǐzuò 仰卧起坐 sit-up	 dònggǎn dānchē 动感 单车 Spinning	 pǔlātí 普拉提 Pilates
 bǎowēnbēi 保温杯 thermos mug	 gǒuqǐ 枸杞 Chinese wolfberry	 shēnhūxī 深呼吸 deep breathing
 píngbǎn zhīchēng 平板 支撑 plank	 yǎlíng 哑铃 dumbbell	 huáchuánjī 划船机 rowing machine

（2）班里有哪些同学想减肥，为他们制订一份减肥计划，并在全班分享。大家评选出“最受欢迎的减肥计划”。

给__________的减肥计划

时间段	要做的事情	不能做的事情
早上		
中午		
下午		
晚上		

（3）神编剧。下面是三个和“减肥”有关的情景，选择一个编写对话，并表演出来。

情景1：你劝说一位想减肥的好友去健身房锻炼。

情景2：你是一家沙拉店的老板，你想让大家来尝尝你的新沙拉。

情景3：你的老板让你把一种新款减肥茶卖掉。

练习对话时，尽可能多地使用下面的词语和句式。

参考词语	体重、胖、身材、吃货、宅、节食、减肥、饮食均衡、必要、保持、控制、热量、戒、代替、甜食、主食、有氧运动、效果、副作用……
参考句式	管住嘴，迈开腿 再说……

第十一课　我办了张健身卡

I got a gym membership

课前热身 Warming up

你知道这是哪儿吗？这是什么卡？

Do you know where it is? What kind of card is this?

生词 New words

1	收费	shōu fèi		to collect fees；to charge
2	季	jì	名	season
3	确实	quèshí	副/形	really；indeed；true；reliable
4	专人	zhuānrén	名	specially assigned person

5	打扫	dǎsǎo	动	to clean; to sweep
6	定期	dìngqī	形	at regular intervals
7	更衣室	gēngyīshì	名	changing room; locker room
8	淋浴间	línyù jiān		shower room
	淋浴	línyù	动	to take a shower
9	器械	qìxiè	名	appliance; instrument
10	齐全	qíquán	形	complete; all in readiness
11	教练	jiàoliàn	名	coach
12	力量	lìliàng	名	strength; power
13	偶尔	ǒu'ěr	副	occasionally
14	拉伸	lā shēn		to stretch
15	肌肉	jīròu	名	muscle
16	的话	dehuà	助	if (used at the end of a conditional clause)
17	下班	xiàbān	动	to go off work
18	尽量	jǐnliàng	副	as much as possible
19	恢复	huīfù	动	to resume; to regain; to recover
20	恰好	qiàhǎo	副	just right
21	开业	kāiyè	动	to start business
22	设施	shèshī	名	installation; facilities
23	恒温	héngwēn	名	constant temperature
24	限	xiàn	动	to set a limit; to limit

25	次数	cìshù	名	number of times; frequency
26	各种各样	gè zhǒng gè yàng		all kinds of; various
27	单车	dānchē	名	bicycle; bike
28	场地	chǎngdì	名	place; space
29	室内	shì nèi		indoor
30	闻	wén	动	to smell
31	股	gǔ	量	a measure word used for strength, smell, etc.; a measure word used for sth. long and narrow
32	汗臭味	hàn chòu wèi		the smell of sweat
33	趁着	chèn zhe		take advantage of; under the cover of
34	尽管	jǐnguǎn	连	even though; in spite of
35	早日	zǎorì	副	at an early date; soon

专名 Proper nouns

动感单车	Dònggǎn dānchē	Spinning (indoor cycling)

课文 Text

课文1 Text 1

米亚：你是不是常常去健身房锻炼？

阿里：是啊，我办了一张健身卡。

米亚：怎么收费的？

阿里：我办的是季卡，一个月300块左右，不但可以健身，还可以游泳。如果买年卡，价格应该更优惠。

米亚：价格确实不贵。环境怎么样？

阿里：环境还可以，有专人打扫，游泳池也会定期换水，还有更衣室、淋浴间什么的。

米亚：器械齐全吗？教练怎么样？

阿里：各种器械都有，也比较新。教练都很有耐心，也很专业。

米亚：你去健身房练什么？

阿里：我一般做一些力量练习，偶尔上瑜伽课拉伸肌肉，天气好的话，每周也会游一两次泳。

米亚：那里人多不多？

阿里：挺多的，不过大部分人都是下班后去健身房，我喜欢在人少的时候去，所以我尽量下午去，或者晚上晚一点儿去。

米亚：离学校远不远？

阿里：不远，就在学校附近。

米亚：下次我跟你一起去看看，我也想办一张卡。

课文② Text 2

来中国以后，我胖了许多。为了恢复以前的好身材，我决定健身减肥。学校附近恰好有一家健身房刚刚开业，价格优惠，设施比较齐全，还有恒温游泳池。我去办了一张健身卡，一年两千多块，不限次数，随时可以去。所以我打算以后只要有时间，就去锻炼。

健身房里有各种各样的健身项目，跑步、瑜伽、跳舞、动感单车……就是健身的场地有点儿小，下班后去健身的人很多，室内空气不太流通，偶尔会闻到一股汗臭味，让人很不舒服。我打算以后趁着下午人少的时候去，先做力量练习，再跑步，最后游一会儿泳。尽管最近有点儿忙，我还是坚持每周去两三次，希望能早日减肥成功。

语言知识 Language guidelines

知识① Tip 1

“……的话”

“天气好的话，每周也会游一两次泳”

“……的话”用在条件句中，表示某种条件的假设，可以和“如果”或者“要是”一起用，意思不变。例如：

“……的话” is used in a conditional sentence to indicate a certain assumption of a condition. It can be used together with “如果” or “要是”, with the same meaning. E. g. ,

（1）不下雨的话，我们就去逛街。

（2）如果你们去的话，我也去。

（3）要是累的话，休息一下吧！

知识 2 Tip 2

“恰好”

“学校附近恰好有一家健身房刚刚开业”

1. 副词“恰好”指正好在某个点上，即时间不早不晚、空间不前不后、数量不多不少的意思。例如：

The adverb “恰好” refers to a certain perfect point in terms of timing, position or quantity. E. g. ,

（1）A：这些一共 25 块钱。

　　B：恰好我手机上有 25 块，我用手机付吧！

（2）A：我想去图书馆借一下《中文》这本书。

　　B：我恰好有这本书，我借给你。

（3）八个人一桌，我们十六个人恰好坐两桌。

2. “恰好”后面常跟数量词，数量词前加“是”“有”，意思相同。例如：

“恰好” is often followed by a numeral-classifier compound. Which can be preceded by “是” or “有”, without distorting the meaning. E. g. ,

（1）不多不少，这儿恰好（是）十个苹果。

（2）我来中国恰好（有）两个月了。

（3）加上这件东西，恰好 100 元。

3. “恰好”还可以加形容词。例如：

“恰好” can also be used with an adjective. E. g. ,

(1) 这双鞋子不大不小，恰好合适。

(2) 他们俩的性格恰好相反，一个内向，一个外向。

(3) 这个箱子装这些东西恰好够。

用法对比：“恰好”和“正好”

Compare：“恰好” and “正好”

“恰好”在作副词时，与“正好”的用法相同，但比“正好”更强调事情的巧合性。“恰好”一般不能作补语或谓语，“正好”可以。例如：

As an adverb，“恰好” is used in the same way as “正好”，but it lays more emphasis on the coincidence than the latter. “恰好” generally cannot be used as a complement or predicate，but “正好” can. E. g. ,

(1) 我钱包丢了，学生卡正好在里面，麻烦了。(恰好)

(2) 他没站稳，正好我站在旁边，他想扶我，结果我俩都摔倒了。(恰好)

(3) 我想抽时间把东西还你，正好遇到你爱人，就把东西给他了。(恰好)

(4) 这儿空着，把桌子放这儿正好。(* 恰好)

(5) 你俩来得正好，我刚想找人帮我搬东西。(* 恰好)

知识❸ Tip 3

“就是”

“就是健身的场地有点儿小”

副词“就是”有确定范围、排除其他的作用。后面常加名词、动词或小句。例如：

The adverb “就是” has the function of determining the scope and excluding others. It is often followed by a noun, a verb, or a clause. E. g. ,

（1）这些水果我都喜欢，就是不喜欢榴莲。

（2）桌上是有很多东西，可是就是没有你的手机。

（3）这个孩子挺聪明的，就是有点儿懒。

知识❹ Tip 4

“趁着”

“我打算以后趁着下午人少的时候去”

“趁着”表示利用条件或机会，后面可以加双音节或多音节的名词和形容词，也可以加动词短语和句子。例如：

“趁着” means taking advantage of a condition or an opportunity. Nouns and adjectives with two or more syllables can be added after it, besides verb phrases and sentences. E. g. ,

（1）趁着现在有空，我把房间打扫一下。

（2）他想趁着年轻多学一点东西。

（3）小偷趁着我不注意，把我的钱包偷走了。

知识5 Tip 5

“尽管……，还是/但是/可是……”

“尽管最近有点儿忙，我还是坚持每周去两三次”

连词“尽管”表示姑且承认某种事实，后一小句常用“但是”“可是”“然而”“可”“还是”“仍然”“却”等表示转折的连词和它呼应。“尽管”也可用在后一小句。例如：

“尽管” is used to concede a fact (reluctantly in most cases), which is echoed by adversative conjunctions like “但是”“可是”“然而”“可”“还是”“仍然” and “却” in the latter clause. “尽管” can also be used in the latter clause. E. g. ,

(1) 尽管工资不高，但是我喜欢这个工作。

(2) 尽管老师说了半天，可是我还是不明白。

(3) 爷爷身体十分健康，尽管他已经 80 多岁了。

用法对比：“尽管”“不管”和“即使”

Compare: “尽管”“不管” and “即使”

“尽管”“不管”和“即使”都是连词，用于前一个小句，表示复句中的让步关系。

“尽管”“不管” and “即使” are conjunctions which can be used in the preceding clause to indicate the concessional relationship in a complex sentence.

1. “不管”用于条件句里表示“无条件”，即在任何情况下都是如此，与“不论”“无论”相当。“不管”后面的词语多是有选择的，常跟“形容词+形容词”，不常跟“是否”“与否”“如何”等文言词。

例如：

“不管” is used in conditional sentences to indicate “unconditional”, which means the result remains the same under any circumstances. It is equivalent to “不论”“无论”. Most words following “不管” are in the pattern of “adjective + adjective” providing options, while written words such as “是否”“与否” and “如何” are not commonly used in this case. E. g. ,

（1）不管早晚，他都会来的。

（2）孩子不管大小，都是妈妈的宝贝。

（3）我不管忙不忙，都会去健身房。

（4）不管怎么说，你的手机找到了就好。

2. “即使”用于假设、转折、让步句，表示的情况是假设或者极端的，与“就是”相当，后面的词语不能是有选择性的。例如：

Similar to “就是”, “即使” is used in the hypothetical, contrasting, and concessional sentences, indicating that the situation is hypothetical or extreme, and no options should be provided. E. g. ,

不管	即使
不管天晴还是下雨，他都不迟到。	即使刮台风，他也不迟到。
我不管忙不忙，都会去健身房。	我即使特别忙，也会去健身房。
不管你多大，你都是妈妈的孩子。	即使你长大了，你也是妈妈的孩子。

3. “尽管”与“即使”相当，只是表示的情况是一种事实。例如：

“尽管”is equivalent to“即使”，except that it indicates a factual situation. E. g.，

尽管	即使
尽管今天刮台风，他都没迟到。 （真的刮台风了）	即使明天刮台风，他也不迟到。 （不一定真的刮台风）
尽管我特别忙，我还是去了健身房。 （真的特别忙）	即使我特别忙，也会去健身房。 （不一定真的忙）
尽管你长大了，你还是妈妈的孩子。 （真的长大了）	即使你长大了，你还是妈妈的孩子。 （不一定真的长大）

练习 Exercises

1. **词语搭配**。Complete the phrases.

打扫__________　　拉伸__________　　恢复__________

__________器械　　__________教练　　__________力量

__________设施　　室内__________　　__________单车

定期__________　　__________齐全　　专业__________

2. 选词填空。Choose the right words to fill in the blanks.

季卡　定期　齐全　专业　减肥　室内　股　流通　恢复

（1）我在健身房办了一张__________，价格挺便宜的。

（2）这个房间的空气一点儿也不__________，把窗户打开吧！

（3）你已经很瘦了，为什么还要__________？

（4）打完球以后，我身上有一__________汗味。

（5）他__________去医院检查身体。

（6）在很多国家，__________不可以抽烟。

（7）适当的运动能帮助病人__________健康。

（8）那个超市里的商品很__________，有时间咱们去逛逛。

（9）婚礼上，新郎新娘请了__________的摄影师帮他们拍视频。

3. 改错句。Correct the sentences.

（1）这次表演有跳舞专人。

____

（2）我们宿舍有专人维修师傅。

____

（3）动物园的动物齐全。

____

（4）朋友开业新咖啡店。

____

（5）这双鞋子我穿得恰好。

____

（6）这家博物馆参观的限是 120 分钟。

____

4．组句。 Rearrange the words to form a sentence.

（1）有　健身房　附近　一家　恰好　开业　我家

____

（2）以后　选择　去　大部分人　锻炼　都　下班

____

（3）打算　趁着　人少　我　去　的时候

____

（4）会　汗臭味　偶尔　闻到　我　一股

____

（5）健身　各种各样　健身房　有　的　项目

____

（6）的　恢复　好身材　我　了　以前

____

5．完成句子。 Complete the sentences.

（1）A：你可以坐高铁去上海。

B：______________________________。（确实）

（2）我哥哥很懒，______________________________。（偶尔）

（3）A：明天去踢足球怎么样？

B：______________________________。（的话）

（4）______________________________，我们可以早点儿去。（的话）

（5）如果事情办得快，______________________________。（尽量）

(6) 为了学好中文，______________________________。(尽量)

(7) 休息了两个小时后，__________________________。(恢复)

(8) 你刚才说的话，______________________________。(恰好)

(9) ______________________________，我们快点走吧。(趁着)

(10) ____________________________，他还是努力学习。(尽管)

(11) 祝你______________________________________。(早日)

6. 根据课文回答问题。Answer the questions according to the text.

课文 1

(1) 米亚想跟阿里去看什么？为什么？

____

(2) 阿里办的是什么卡？怎么办卡更优惠？

____

(3) 阿里喜欢什么时候去健身房？为什么？

____

(4) 阿里一般在健身房做什么运动？

____

课文 2

(1) “我”为什么办了一张健身卡？

____

(2) “我”对这家健身房满意吗？从哪儿看得出来？

____

（3）“我”有什么不满意的地方？“我”打算怎么办？

____

7．**健身房挑战赛**。Challenge fitness programs.

（1）下面是什么健身项目？把它们的中文名字写下来。

 a. ______________ swimming	 b. ______________ yoga	 c. ______________ spinning
 d. ______________ body building exercise	 e. ______________ dumbbell	 f. ______________ barbell
 g. ______________ running machine	 h. ______________ step	 i. ______________ rowing machine

（2）看图片，完成对话。

A：________________

B：________________

A：________________

B：________________

A：________________

B：________________

A：________________

B：________________

A：________________

B：________________

A：________________

B：________________

A：________________

B：________________

A：________________

B：________________

（3）金牌推销员。

全班同学分为两部分：一部分是“想办健身卡的人”，另一部分是不同健身房的“推销员”。角色由老师随机分配，同时每人得到下列三组词卡中的一组。

参考词卡
A 组词卡：价格便宜、空气流通、锻炼力量、开业优惠、动感单车
B 组词卡：场地宽敞、健身项目、拉伸肌肉、汗臭味、恒温泳池
C 组词卡：设施齐全、教练专业、出汗减肥、恢复身材、瑜伽舞蹈

同学拿到词卡后，“推销员”自由走动，向“想办健身卡的人”介绍自己的健身房，“想办健身卡的人”一边听介绍一边提问题，双方须用完手中的全部词语。介绍完毕，“想办健身卡的人”选择想去的健身房，获得办卡人数最多的推销员评为“金牌推销员”。

8．小练笔。 Writing.

如果我有一笔钱的话，我要建一个这样的健身房……（不少于100个字）

第十二课　你看足球比赛吗

Do you watch the football match

课前热身 Warming up

你喜欢看足球比赛吗？说一说你们国家的足球情况。

Do you like watching football matches? Tell us something about football in your country.

生词 New words

1	熬夜	áoyè	动	to stay up late
2	球赛	qiúsài	名	ball game
3	时差	shíchā	名	time difference；jet lag
4	直播	zhíbō	动	to have live broadcast

5	半夜	bànyè	名	midnight；half of a night
6	一连	yìlián	副	in a row；in succession
7	守门员	shǒuményuán	名	goalkeeper
8	球员	qiúyuán	名	player
9	首都	shǒudū	名	capital
10	俱乐部	jùlèbù	名	club
11	成员	chéngyuán	名	member
12	反正	fǎnzhèng	副	anyway；in any cases；since
13	闺蜜	guīmì	名	bosom friend；ladybro
14	帅哥	shuài gē		handsome boy
15	美称	měichēng	名	laudatory title；good name
16	全球	quánqiú	名	the whole world；globe
17	影响力	yǐngxiǎng lì		influence
	影响	yǐngxiǎng	动/名	to affect；influence
18	集体	jítǐ	名	collective；group
19	有名	yǒumíng	形	well-known；famous
20	举办	jǔbàn	动	to conduct；to hold
21	届	jiè	量	session（of a conference）；year（of graduation）
22	受到	shòu dào		to receive；to accept
23	人民	rénmín	名	people
24	广泛	guǎngfàn	形	wide-ranging
25	关注	guānzhù	动	to pay close attention to
26	期间	qījiān	名	period

27	通常	tōngcháng	副/形	usually; generally; usual; normal
28	聚集	jùjí	动	to gather
29	配	pèi	动	to match; to compound

专名 Proper nouns

1	世界杯	Shìjiè bēi	World Cup
2	英格兰*	Yīnggélán	England
3	C 罗*	C Luó	Cristiano Ronaldo (a football player)
4	葡萄牙*	Pútáoyá	Portugal
5	皇家马德里*	Huángjiā Mǎdélǐ	Real Madrid
	马德里*	Mǎdélǐ	Madrid
6	欧冠*	Ōu Guàn	UEFA Champions League
7	英超*	Yīng Chāo	FA Premier League
8	西甲*	Xī Jiǎ	La Liga; Division A League Matches of Spanish Football
9	意甲*	Yì Jiǎ	Lega Serie A
10	德甲*	Dé Jiǎ	German Bundesliga
11	欧洲	Ōuzhōu	Europe
12	美洲	Měizhōu	America

课文 Text

课文1 Text 1

王乐乐：你的眼睛怎么这么红？

林　一：昨晚熬夜看球赛，今天早上又得早起，怎么能不红呢？

王乐乐：什么球赛？为什么要熬夜看？

林　一：世界杯。由于时差，直播时间都在半夜，只好熬夜看了。

王乐乐：昨晚是哪两个球队比赛？

林　一：西班牙对英格兰，西班牙一连踢进三个球，超级精彩，不过，英格兰的守门员也挺厉害的……对了，你看足球比赛吗？

王乐乐：时间不太晚的话我也会看。西班牙有个叫 C 罗的球员，踢球的时候真是太帅了。

林　一：C 罗是葡萄牙的，你搞错了。

王乐乐：他不是皇家马德里的球员吗？马德里不是西班牙的首都吗？

林　一：皇家马德里是俱乐部，俱乐部的成员可以是其他国家的。

王乐乐：不管他是西班牙的还是葡萄牙的，反正我就爱看他的比赛，我的闺蜜也喜欢。

林　一：唉，女生看球和男生就是不一样。

王乐乐：有什么不一样？

林　一：我们看的是比赛，你们看的是帅哥。

王乐乐：哈哈，说得对。

课文❷ Text 2

足球一直有着“世界第一运动”的美称，是全球最有影响力的集体运动。世界上有名的足球比赛事有很多，像欧冠、英超、西甲、意甲、德甲等，尤其是每四年举办一届的世界杯，更是受到世界各国人民的广泛关注。

虽然中国的足球水平不算高，但是有不少中国人喜欢踢足球，爱看足球比赛。特别是在世界杯期间，因为世界杯通常在欧洲或者美洲举办，跟中国有时差，比赛直播时间常常在半夜，球迷们为了看直播晚上不睡觉，很多人聚集在一起熬夜看球，这时候当然还要配上小龙虾和啤酒。

如果有时差，你会熬夜看球吗？你有没有喜欢的足球运动员？你的国家足球踢得怎么样？

语言知识 Language guidelines

知识❶ Tip 1

教学视频

“一连”

“西班牙一连踢进三个球”

副词“一连”表示动作连续不断或情况连续发生，强调数量多或时间长，常用“一连＋动词＋数量词”，也用“一连＋数量词＋（都）＋动词”。例如：

The adverb “一连” modifies actions or situations that occur continuously, suggesting a large quantity or a long time. It is commonly used as “一连＋verb＋numeral-classifier compound” or “一连＋numeral-classifier compound + （都） + verb”. E. g. ,

（1）一连下了三天雨，路上都是水。

（2）为了买到和以前一样的耳机，他一连去了四五家店。

（3）终于拿到了 HSK4 级证书，她高兴得一连几天没睡好觉。

（4）我一连七天都在家里上网课。

知识❷ Tip 2

“反正”

“反正我就爱看他的比赛”

1. 副词“反正”强调在任何情况下都不改变结论或结果，上文常有“不管”“无论”或表示正反两种情况的词语，多用在主语前。例如：

The adverb “反正” emphasizes that the conclusion or result should not be changed under any circumstances. The words “不管” “无论” as well as words indicating both positive and negative situations are often used in front of it. It is often used before the subject. E. g. ,

（1）不管你去不去，反正我要去。

（2）无论你怎么说，反正我不同意。

（3）你喜不喜欢不重要，反正我已经买了。

（4）你也可以，他也可以，反正我们班要有一个人去参加。

2. 有时“反正”也用在前一分句，作为后一分句的理由，或指明情况，语气较强，多用在动词、形容词或主语前。例如：

Sometimes “反正” is also used in the former clause to introduce the reason for the latter clause or to indicate a situation with a heavy tone. It is often used before a verb, an adjective, or the subject. E. g. ,

（1）我反正要出去，可以顺便帮你拿快递。

（2）反正不远，我们走路去吧！

（3）反正我不会同意，你说什么也没用。

知识3 Tip 3

“有着”

“足球一直有着‘世界第一运动’的美称”

“有着”即“有＋着”，常用作书面语，意思是“存在着”“具有”，后面可以加具体名词，也可以加抽象名词，比如习惯、目的、爱好、感情等，但是都不能直接加在“有着”之后，名词前必须有修饰成分。例如：

“有着” is often used in written language, meaning “exist”. It can be followed by a specific noun or an abstract noun, such as words denoting habits, purposes, hobbies, emotions, etc. However, the noun cannot be directly added after “有着”. There must be a modifier before it. E. g. ,

（1）我们学校留学生很多，所以有着“小联合国”的称号。

（2）他的足球踢得特别好，他在球队中有着重要的地位。

（3）老爷爷和他的家人有着很深的感情。

（4）听到他的故事，我的心里有着说不出的难过。

知识④ Tip 4

“受到”

“受到世界各国人民的广泛关注”

1. “受到”表示接受、得到，可以带名词、动词、小句作宾语。例如：

The word “受到” means “to accept, to receive” and can take a noun, a verb, or a clause as the object. E. g. ,

（1）受到父母的影响，我对中国文化十分感兴趣。

（2）希望所有的孩子都能受到好的教育。

（3）商店免费送菜上门，受到大家的欢迎。

2. “受到”还常常表示遭受不幸的事情或损害，后面常加否定意义的词语，可以带名词、动词。例如：

The word “受到” also means “to suffer from something bad or to be harmed”, and is often followed by a negative word. It can take a noun or a verb as the object. E. g. ,

（1）他上课睡觉，受到了老师的批评。

（2）他酒后开车，受到了处罚。

（3）事故中两辆汽车都受到了严重损坏。

练习 Exercises

1. 词语搭配。 Complete the phrases.

举办________ ________直播 ________精彩

________俱乐部 ________联赛 关注________

影响________ ________广泛 受到________

2. 选词填空。 Choose the right words to fill in the blanks.

影响 聚集 期间 不管 一连 反正 尤其 举办 通常

（1）________她爱不爱我，我都会一直爱她。

（2）我________每周都去打网球，但是这周真的没有空。

（3）我太渴了，________喝了三杯水。

（4）别的人去不去，我不知道，________老师一定会去。

（5）我哥哥打算下个月在国外________婚礼。

（6）每周五晚很多留学生________在这儿举行语言派对。

（7）他喜欢中国，________喜欢中国美食。

（8）昨晚楼上太吵了，________了我睡觉。

（9）医生告诉我，身体恢复________，不要吃太辣太咸的食物。

3. 改错句。 Correct the sentences.

（1）昨天我熬夜睡觉。

____

（2）昨天半夜我看直播篮球比赛。

____

(3) 老师举办汉字课。

(4) 他是一个很尤其的学生。

(5) 反正遇到什么困难，我们都要互相帮助。

(6) 反正你们相不相信，不管我相信。

(7) 我受到了你的礼物。

(8) 班长一分钟十个一连做了动作。

4. **组句**。Rearrange the words to form a sentence.

(1) 是　影响力　集体运动　全球　最有　足球　的

(2) 关注　广泛　受到　这个问题　全国人民　的

(3) 时差　半夜　直播时间　在　由于　都

(4) 足球比赛　什么　喜欢　我　都　不管　看

(5) 世界杯　欧洲　举办　通常　在　或者　美洲

5. **完成句子**。Complete the sentences.

（1）______________________，我的衣服每天都是湿的。（一连）

（2）我______________________，现在太饱了，吃不下了。（一连）

（3）A：我周末打算去图书馆复习，图书馆几点开门？

B：____。（通常）

（4）不管别人去不去，_______________________________。（反正）

（5）随便你怎么说，_________________________________。（反正）

（6）他常常帮助大家，_______________________________。（受到）

（7）__________________________，她看起来十分难过。（受到）

（8）长时间看手机对身体不好，_______________________。（尤其）

6. **根据课文回答问题**。Answer the questions according to the text.

课文 1

（1）林一的眼睛为什么很红？

____

（2）昨晚是什么球赛？比赛情况怎么样？

____

（3）王乐乐喜欢哪一个足球运动员？为什么？

____

课文 2

（1）足球有什么好听的名字？为什么？

____

（2）世界杯是什么？

____

（3）世界杯期间，中国球迷怎么看球？为什么？

____

7. 球迷俱乐部。 Organize football fans club event.

（1）下面这些词语，你知道它们的意思吗？给同学们介绍一下。

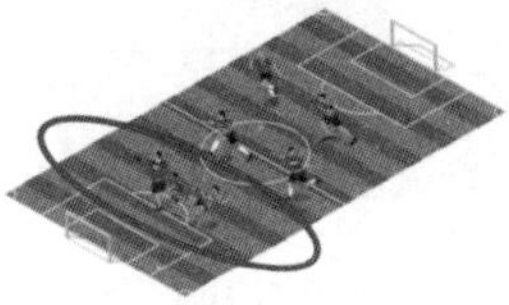 qiánfēng 前锋 forward	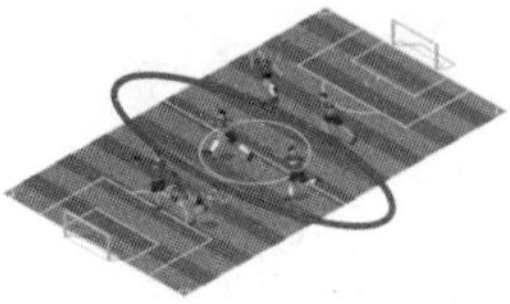 zhōng chǎng 中场 midfield	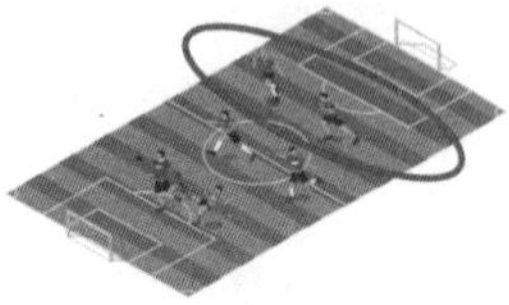 hòu chǎng 后场 backfield
 shǒuményuán 守门员 goalkeeper	 jiàoliàn 教练 coach	 cáipàn 裁判 referee

（续上表）

 shèmén 射门 shoot	 chǎnqiú 铲球 slide tackle	 fànguī 犯规 foul
 diǎnqiú 点球 penalty kick	 píngjú 平局 draw	 jiāshísài 加时赛 extra time

（2）足球小知识。

a. 足球场的形状是____ A. 正方形　B. 长方形	e. 加时赛中间休息吗？ A. 休息　B. 不休息
b. 足球比赛双方各有多少人？ A. 10 人　B. 11 人	f. 点球赛有几轮？ A. 4 轮　B. 5 轮
c. 足球赛的比赛时长是多久？ A. 90 分钟　B. 100 分钟	g. 一场比赛会有几个裁判？ A. 3 个　B. 4 个
d. 加时赛的时长是多久？ A. 30 分钟　B. 40 分钟	h. 比赛中每队最多可换几个人？ A. 3 个　B. 5 个

（3）王牌解说员。

看一段足球比赛的视频，同学们一边听一边记录视频中的足球解说词，老师随机选几位同学上台，其他同学选择一句视频中的解说词发问。台上的同学根据听到的解说词表演动作，做对动作最多的同学赢。

8．小练笔。Writing.

写一写“我最喜欢的一项运动”。（不少于100个字）

参考答案 Answers

第一课　你带钱包了吗

1.（答案合理即可，以下供参考）

手机	银行卡	手机	密码
扫	功能	支付	老师
考试	水电费	成绩	手机

2.

（1）支付　（2）成为　（3）完成　（4）随着

（5）设置　（6）值得　（7）甚至　（8）绑定

3.

（1）其他　（2）其他/别的　（3）别的　（4）其他/别的

（5）其他　（6）其他

4.（答案合理即可，以下供参考）

（1）我从没有见过中国的长城。

（2）随着中文水平的提高，我越来越喜欢中国的文化。

（3）今天不忙，我要洗衣服。

（4）他十分有钱。

（5）你在学校做什么工作？

（6）茶有很多种，红茶是其中一种。

（7）飞机里有三百多人，其中有一个是我的朋友。

5.（答案合理即可，以下供参考）

（1）在微信首页的右上角有一个加号。

（2）你先要设置付款密码。

（3）手机已经成为人们生活中重要的伙伴。

（4）最值得一提的是支付功能。

（5）随着技术的提高，生活越来越方便。

（6）人们担心手机支付的安全问题。

6.（答案合理即可，以下供参考）

（1）我从没用过手机付钱

（2）比如北京、上海、广州等

（3）其中茶文化最有意思

（4）值得一提的是支付功能

（5）你不要告诉其他人

（6）甚至没有时间休息

（7）不仅交通方便，还很漂亮

（8）随着交通越来越方便

7.（答案合理即可，以下供参考）

课文 1

（1）阿里忘记带钱包了。他可以用手机来付钱。

（2）微信或支付宝先要绑定银行卡，然后设置付款密码。付钱的时候，打开微信或支付宝，选择“扫一扫”，扫一下付款二维码，就可以付钱了。

课文 2

（1）刚开始的时候，很多人不习惯用手机支付，担心手机支付不安全。

（2）现在，随着技术的提高，越来越多的人对手机支付已经很放心了。

（3）买东西付钱，交话费、水电费，给别人转账等。

（4）打电话、听音乐、拍照、看电影等。

（5）（略）

8.（略）

9.（略）

第二课　出门靠朋友

1.（答案合理即可，以下供参考）

家人	同学	困难	大雨	朋友
新生活	遇到	说	考试	

2.

(1) 幸运　(2) 适应　(3) 顺利　(4) 帮助

(5) 互相　(6) 恨不得　(7) 摔　(8) 受伤

(9) 回国　(10) 靠

3.（答案合理即可，以下供参考）

(1) 我们应该关心自己的分数。

(2) 这本书不仅不难也很有意思。

(3) 最近太累了，我恨不得马上休息不工作。

(4) 刚来的时候，我一点儿也不适应这里的生活。

(5) 昨天晚上我摔倒了，我的手受伤了。

(6) 亲爱的爸爸妈妈，你们身体怎么样？

(7) 他们一切事情都很顺利。

(8) 我买了一本中文书，还要买其他书。

4.（答案合理即可，以下供参考）

(1) 听说班长昨天晚上摔伤了。

(2) 他平时帮助大家学习中文。

(3) 下课后，其他同学来医院看我。

(4) 我的中文说得流利着呢！

(5) 一遇到困难，我就恨不得马上回国。

5.（答案合理即可，以下供参考）

(1) 靠中国朋友的帮助，我每天练习中文

(2) 说实话，我觉得非常方便

（3）恨不得 24 小时都玩手机

（4）一下课就回家

（5）一切都不顺利

（6）好朋友会互相关心、互相帮助

（7）对了，你能帮我买一瓶水吗

（8）幸运的是精彩的节目还没开始

6. （答案合理即可，以下供参考）

课文 1

（1）“太阳从西边出来了”是说不可能发生的事情发生了。艾文这么说，是因为今天班长没来上课。

（2）班长摔伤了，她晚上爬楼梯的时候，灯太暗了，不小心摔下来了。

（3）同学们打算一下课就去医院看班长。因为班长平时总是帮助大家，现在班长有困难了，同学们觉得应该帮助她。

课文 2

（1）安娜刚来中国的时候，一点儿也不习惯，中文不好，又没有朋友，每次遇到困难，都恨不得马上回国。

（2）因为安娜的班主任、同学都很关心她，现在她已经适应了中国的生活，每天都过得很开心，中文也说得很流利。

7. （略）

8. （略）

第三课　我的脚扭伤了

1.（答案合理即可，以下供参考）

片子	足球	箱子	问
膏药	身体	面膜	受伤
服药			

2.

（1）倒霉	（2）走动	（3）按时	（4）片子
（5）正常	（6）还	（7）厉害	（8）结果

3.（答案合理即可，以下供参考）

A.

（1）还不错	（2）还好	（3）还可以	（4）还便宜
（5）还少	（6）还行		

B.

（1）都晚上 12 点了，你怎么还在玩手机？

（2）他都 40 岁了，还没有结婚。

（3）你都是大学生了，还喜欢小孩子的玩具吗？

（4）我们都等了 2 个小时了，他为什么还没有来？

（5）你都吃了 3 碗面条了，还没有吃饱吗？

C.

（1）他的头疼得厉害。

（2）他的牙齿疼得厉害。

（3）他咳嗽咳得厉害。

（4）他拉肚子拉得厉害。

（5）他的脚肿得厉害。

（6）他发烧烧得厉害。

4.（答案合理即可，以下供参考）

（1）我喜欢拍漂亮的风景。

（2）以前买的裤子，现在有点儿短。

（3）孩子三岁的时候就可以走路了。

（4）我的脚扭伤了，所以老板让我在家里休息两天再上班。

（5）我喜欢喝牛奶，所以我的骨头很强壮。

5.（答案合理即可，以下供参考）

（1）结果衣服都淋湿了

（2）结果拉肚子了

（3）结果第二天交不了作业

（4）按时到教室

（5）的病很严重

（6）可以正常走路了

（7）要认真检查

（8）都来问老师问题

6.（答案合理即可，以下供参考）

课文 1

（1）林一去了医院，因为他的脚扭伤了，疼得厉害。

（2）不严重，因为医生说“还好，没伤到骨头”。

课文 2

（1）林一最近特别倒霉，先是钱包丢了，然后是写完的作业找不到了，上个星期踢足球的时候，他的脚踝又扭伤了，结果不能正常走路。

（2）林一贴了“我”给他买的膏药以后，脚踝肿得更厉害了，所以“我”陪他去医院检查。

（3）不用，因为医生检查了以后说没有什么大问题。

（4）医生检查了以后说没有什么大问题，给他开了两种药，告诉他怎么服药，怎么用喷雾，还告诉他不要经常走动，要多休息，两个星期以后就没事儿了。

7.

（1）（略）

（2）挂号　内科　病历　检查　化验　交费　药房

8.（略）

第四课　租房

1.（答案合理即可，以下供参考）

房	朋友	学校	公司
空气	房屋	欢迎	空调
保护	便宜	交通	好

2.

（1）挑剔　（2）吵　（3）套　（4）便利

（5）宽敞　（6）稍微　（7）阳光　（8）谨慎

（9）周围

3.（答案合理即可，以下供参考）

（1）放着几本书

（2）摆着一些桌子和椅子

（3）有很多箱子

（4）站着五个人

（5）走下来一个人

（6）开过来一辆车

4.（答案合理即可，以下供参考）

（1）我买了很多东西，花了很多钱。

（2）老师对不起，我会稍微迟到几分钟。

（3）明天要考试，我稍微有一点儿担心。

（4）我和朋友一起合交电费。

（5）我去学校食堂买一份饭。

5.（答案合理即可，以下供参考）

（1）不是看书就是写作业

（2）我们的学校可漂亮了

（3）可喜欢了

（4）算便宜的

（5）算认识吧

（6）有几个好朋友算是幸运

（7）能不能稍微说慢一点儿

（8）更不用说会做了

（9）更不用说了解他了

6.（答案合理即可，以下供参考）

课文 1

（1）艾文现在住在学校外面，在北京路附近，他租的房子不算大，五六十平方米，有两个卧室和一个客厅，还有一个大厨房。

（2）他开学前跟朋友一起去了房屋中介，让中介帮他们找的。

课文 2

（1）朋友的公寓离学校稍微有点儿远，他为了不迟到，再也没睡过懒觉了。

（2）他每天先走五分钟的路到小区正门的地铁站，然后坐地铁来学校。

（3）除了交通方便，公寓周围还有超市、银行、商场、医院、公园等，地段好，环境不错，生活很方便。

（4）这套公寓是两室一厅，客厅和阳台都很宽敞，空气流通，阳光很好，每个人都有自己的卧室，上网也很快，住着很舒服。

（5）这套公寓的租金不便宜，一个月要三千多，还要交水电费、网费、物业管理费等。

7.（略）

8.（略）

第五课　中国的高铁真方便

1.（答案合理即可，以下供参考）

改签窗口	高铁座位	准时候车	取票速度
服务体验	点餐服务	尝试高铁	服务满意
选择座位	取票窗口	改签速度	点餐窗口
选择窗口	体验高铁	候车座位	服务准时

2.

（1）选择	（2）尝试	（3）好像	（4）刚好
（5）座位	（6）准时	（7）稳	（8）了不起

3.（答案合理即可，以下供参考）

（1）服务员对我们说，你要点什么餐？

（2）高铁票可以在取票机取。

（3）篮球比赛的票我去取。

（4）我能不能试试你的新手机？

（5）我坐在靠窗的座位上。

（6）我学习中文，另外我也学习英文。

（7）他不仅个子高，还很帅。

（8）爸爸今天不能来，他太忙了，有很多事要做。

（9）每个人都爱他的家人。

4.（答案合理即可，以下供参考）

（1）从广州到深圳只要二十九分钟。

（2）高铁的速度是每小时 300 多公里。

（3）窗外的景色像飞起来了一样。

（4）外国人要去车站窗口用护照取票。

（5）你不用提前两小时去车站候车。

（6）他对高铁的座位非常满意。

5.（答案合理即可，以下供参考）

（1）我很满意

（2）八点准时开始

（3）努力的同学之一

（4）以前大家都一起聊天

（5）另外买了一支笔

（6）刚好下午没课

（7）跟我相比

（8）当时我非常难过

6.（答案合理即可，以下供参考）

课文 1

（1）因为高铁的速度非常快。

（2）高铁的速度是每小时 300 多公里。

（3）阿里喜欢高铁的座位，很宽敞，坐着很舒服，另外还喜欢车上的服务。

（4）可以提前在网上买票，出发前去车站窗口用护照取票；外国人还不能用取票机取票。

课文 2

（1）选择坐高铁。因为跟飞机相比，高铁非常准时，不用提前两个小时去车站候车，另外高铁的座位比较大，走廊也宽敞，坐着舒服。

（2）用手机扫一下座位扶手上的二维码，然后选择喜欢的食物，下单、付款，服务员就会送餐到你的座位上。

（3）因为高铁改签或者退票都很方便。

7.（略）

8.（略）

第六课　坐飞机

1.（答案合理即可，以下供参考）

（1）安检　（2）柜台　（3）传送带　（4）打火机
（5）登机牌　（6）行李箱　（7）登机　（8）空少
（9）电池　（10）充电宝　（11）广播　（12）空姐
（13）照相机　（14）托运　（15）候机

2.（答案合理即可，以下供参考）

手续　写　行李　时间
学校　比赛　下雨　考试
决定

3.

（1）托运　（2）手续　（3）心情　（4）糊涂
（5）服务　（6）忽然　（7）害怕　（8）安检
（9）由于

4.（答案合理即可，以下供参考）

（1）

a. 把车停在停车场

b. 把书放在书架上

c. 把垃圾扔到垃圾桶

d. 把沙发搬到车上

e. 把快递交给客人

f. 把花送给妈妈

g. 把中文翻译成英文

h. 把雪堆成雪人

（2）（略）

5.（答案合理即可，以下供参考）

（1）我们很快登机了。

（2）明天不上课，我们都开心极了。

（3）由于生病了，他不能来上课。

（4）我一进教室就把书包放在桌上。

（5）我把那个快递寄给你了。

（6）我不小心把“午饭”写成“牛饭”了。

（7）我觉得你不能把钱借给他。

（8）我还没把教室的钥匙还给阿姨。

6.（答案合理即可，以下供参考）

（1）把他拦住了

（2）有点糊涂

（3）忽然下雨了

（4）由于临时有事

（5）糟糕透了

（6）你重新说一遍

（7）我临时请假去看妈妈

（8）我们临时决定用碗装蛋糕

7.（答案合理即可，以下供参考）

课文 1

（1）国外。

（2）办理登机牌、托运行李、安检。

（3）他的行李超过了 20 公斤。

课文 2

（1）因为飞机又快又舒服，而且飞机上的空姐、空少服务也十分周到。

（2）因为“我”总是会做点儿糊涂事儿，如忘记带护照，起床起晚了赶不上飞机，托运行李的时候照相机的电池没有拿出来等。

（3）“我”最害怕的是航班临时取消，因为取消以后还得改签或者重新买票。

8.（略）

9.（略）

第七课　学做中国菜

1.（答案合理即可，以下供参考）

（1）打散鸡蛋

（2）把油倒到锅里

（3）给苹果去皮

（4）切西红柿

(5) 倒一点盐

(6) 用勺子舀汤

(7) 切葱花

(8) 炒菜

(9) 把菜盛到盘中

2.(答案合理即可,以下供参考)

菜	出门	菜	饭
汤	做饭	盐	做法
眼睛			

3.

(1) 复杂	(2) 摆	(3) 菜谱	(4) 准备
(5) 适量	(6) 等于	(7) 道	(8) 做法

4.(答案合理即可,以下供参考)

(1) 他们把垃圾扔进垃圾袋。

(2) 他把蛋糕从冰箱里拿出来。

(3) 我把照片挂到墙上。

(4) 他把水倒到杯子里。

(5) 妈妈把菜洗干净。

(6) 小女孩把花瓶打破了。

(7) 我把空调打开吧。

(8) 他把车修好了。

(9) 爷爷把红包给孙子。

（10）请你把名字签上。

5.（答案合理即可，以下供参考）

（1）苹果先去皮，然后切一下。

（2）我把那杯咖啡喝了。

（3）你把衣服洗一下。

（4）我喜欢我的小狗。

（5）他没把昨天的作业做完。

（6）你别把新衣服弄脏了。

（7）他前天坐高铁去了深圳。

6.（答案合理即可，以下供参考）

（1）接着下雨了

（2）接着你说

（3）我准备好了

（4）我准备去广州看看

（5）于是他换了一份新工作

（6）于是做了很多好吃的

（7）你到底去做什么

（8）你到底来不来

7.（答案合理即可，以下供参考）

课文 1

（1）两个西红柿，四个鸡蛋，葱、盐。

（2）先用热水把西红柿烫一下，去皮，然后再把它切成小块，把鸡蛋打散后，加一点儿盐，再把葱切成葱花，接着把油倒在锅里，油热了以后，再把鸡蛋液倒进去，炒一炒就盛出来，然后把西红柿倒进去，放点儿盐炒一炒，再把鸡蛋倒进去，接着和西红柿一起炒，最后放点葱花就做好了。

课文 2

（1）不是太咸就是太淡，不是太甜就是没有味道，因为“我”不知道该放多少调味料。

（2）菜谱上写的“一点儿”“少许”“适量”，这些词的意思都很模糊，“我”不知道到底应该放多少调味料。

（3）（略）

8.（答案合理即可，以下供参考）

（1）

①准备	②干净	③切	④小块
⑤放	⑥锅里	⑦盛	⑧倒
⑨炒	⑩炒	⑪盛	

（2）（略）

9.（略）

第八课　又到“双十一”

1.（答案合理即可，以下供参考）

运动	看书	婚礼	时间
工作	寄	用	管理

商品

2.

（1）仓库　（2）秒杀　（3）性价比　（4）攻略

（5）浪费　（6）经验　（7）促销　（8）当天

（9）堆

3.

A.

（1）满　（2）上　（3）着　（4）光　（5）成

B.（答案合理即可，以下供参考）

（1）只要好好学习，就可以找到好工作。

（2）只有好好学习，才可以找到好工作。

（3）只要你去动物园玩儿，我就去。

（4）只有你去动物园玩儿，才能看到熊猫。

C.（答案合理即可，以下供参考）

（1）对身体不好

（2）要迟到了

（3）被小偷偷走了

（4）你可能会忘记的

（5）妈妈会担心的

D.

（1）接着　（2）接着　（3）继续/接着　（4）接着

（5）继续/接着

E.

（1）每　（2）各　（3）每　（4）各　（5）每

（6）每

4.（答案合理即可，以下供参考）

（1）被我们吃干净了

（2）被他用光了

（3）被他打开了

（4）被我弄脏了

（5）被他关上了

（6）被警察抓住了

5.（答案合理即可，以下供参考）

（1）他散完步了。

（2）他看完电影了。

（3）我和朋友不约而同地在那家店吃饭。

（4）他们俩都不喜欢吃鱼。

（5）妹妹的房间到处都是东西。

6.（答案合理即可，以下供参考）

（1）如果打折

（2）一到 11 月 11 日的凌晨就付钱

（3）只有速度快

（4）不然东西都被别人抢光了

（5）为了买到物美价廉的商品

（6）像山一样高

（7）比实体店便宜了四百多块

（8）便宜是便宜，不过买来以后很多都用不着

7.（答案合理即可，以下仅供参考）

课文1

（1）阿里最近忙着逛淘宝，因为再过几天就是“双十一”了。

（2）“双十一”是中国的购物节。每年的11月11日，淘宝上很多网店都会打折，这时候买东西特别划算。

（3）得提前逛，做好攻略。

（4）“秒杀”是说网购的时候一些商品几秒钟就被人抢光了。想要“秒杀”成功，要提前选好想买的商品，加到购物车里，一到11月11日的凌晨就付钱，只有这样，才能抢到想要的商品。

课文2

（1）快递公司的仓库里，包裹都堆得像山一样高，因为包裹特别多。

（2）因为“双十一”的时候各家电商都会打折，平时需要支付运费的商品也会包邮，人们为了买到物美价廉的商品，都会不约而同地在这一天网购。

（3）“我”不打算买东西，因为“我”觉得一些东西虽然便宜，但是买来以后很多都用不着，是一种浪费。

8.（略）

9.（略）

第九课　送货上门

1.（答案合理即可，以下供参考）

非常流行	登录手机	送货到家	生鲜食品
上门服务	上门时间	网上购物	收货时间
手机购物	送货服务	登录时间	送货上门
送货时间	到家时间	服务时间	服务到家
购物时间	非常时间	非常服务	

2.

（1）催　（2）下载　（3）登录　（4）上门

（5）懒　（6）确定　（7）立刻　（8）选择

（9）高效

3.（答案合理即可，以下供参考）

A.

（1）连小朋友也认识这个字。

（2）他不会说中文，连“你好”也不会说。

（3）很多人不相信他说的话，连他的爸爸妈妈也不相信他说的话。

B.

（1）无论老师还是同学，都喜欢他。

（2）她无论中文还是英文，都说得很流利。

（3）他无论学习还是运动，都很好。

C.

（1）这本书我不是去书店买的，而是在网上买的。

（2）他不是来中国旅游，而是来中国看朋友。

（3）他周末不是去图书馆看书，而是去踢球。

4.（答案合理即可，以下供参考）

（1）我去超市买新鲜的鱼。

（2）不好意思，我不在宿舍，可以明天取快递吗？

（3）今天下午快递小哥把我的东西送过来。

（4）当我回国时，我一定去你家做客。

（5）我三年以内就可以毕业了。

（6）这道题很难，连老师也不会做。

（7）我妈妈说我是最聪明的孩子。

（8）我不是中国人，但是我看起来像中国人。

（9）他被警察罚款五百块钱，因为开车开得太快了。

（10）这种药对身体很有效。

5.（答案合理即可，以下供参考）

（1）麻烦你帮我开一下门。

（2）现在网上买菜非常流行。

（3）我下单才半个多小时就到了。

（4）上门服务让现代人变得越来越懒。

（5）快递让人们的生活变得高效。

6.（答案合理即可，以下供参考）

（1）我连一口也吃不下

（2）许多人去公园散步

（3）重量要在 20 公斤以内

（4）他立刻跑出教室

（5）无论什么时候

（6）将在明晚 8 点开始

（7）不是认真听课，而是玩手机

（8）从价格来看

（9）从我买的东西来看

（10）另一方面我不常拍照

7.（答案合理即可，以下供参考）

课文 1

（1）快递来了。

（2）蔬菜和水果。

（3）和淘宝差不多，下载买菜的 App，用手机登录，选择自己想买的东西，然后确定取件的时间，最后付钱就可以了。

课文 2

（1）简单又高效，因为有方便快捷的快递服务。

（2）也许在不远的未来，把快递包裹送上门的将不是快递小哥，而是智能化的无人机和无人车。

（3）（略）

8.（略）

9.（略）

第十课　减肥

1.（答案合理即可，以下供参考）

（1）胖　（2）主食　（3）夏装　（4）甜食
（5）宅女　（6）身材　（7）饼干　（8）节食
（9）有氧运动　（10）体重　（11）升温　（12）饮食均衡

2.（答案合理即可，以下供参考）

烟　体重　饮食　朋友
减少　保持　饮食　主食
安静

3.

（1）至少　（2）终于　（3）必要　（4）增加
（5）均衡　（6）随便　（7）简单　（8）控制
（9）保持

4.

（1）起来　（2）起来　（3）下去　（4）起来
（5）下去　（6）下来　（7）出来　（8）下来
（9）出来　（10）出来　（11）起来　（12）出来

5.（答案合理即可，以下供参考）

（1）他的身体健康。

（2）教室的温度升高了。

（3）服务员，这个碗有点儿脏，请问能换一个吗？

（4）我用这件衣服代替那件脏衣服。

（5）下个月我还要学习中文。

（6）我明年打算住在中国。

（7）我以为他是中国人，他竟然是法国人。

（8）他不常生气，每天都很开心。

6.（答案合理即可，以下供参考）

（1）没必要减肥

（2）竟然穿不上了

（3）说到减肥

（4）随便吃东西

（5）甜食戒了

（6）每周至少去三次

（7）肯定不能坚持下去

（8）恐怕会有副作用

7.（答案合理即可，以下供参考）

课文 1

（1）因为她的体重又增加了，她想要节食减肥。

（2）不对，因为她觉得米亚不胖，没必要减肥，另外她觉得节食对身体不好。

（3）她以前比现在重10多斤；均衡饮食，多运动，每周至少去三次健身房。

课文2

（1）以前能穿上的裤子现在穿不下了。

（2）“管住嘴”就是节食减肥，“迈开腿”就是运动减肥。节食减肥，要控制饮食，少吃高热量的食品，戒奶茶、戒甜食、戒炸鸡……用蔬菜和水果代替主食。运动减肥，要多做有氧运动，比如跑步、游泳、骑车，勤锻炼身体。

（3）不容易，因为只靠节食减肥对身体不好，运动减肥需要长时间坚持才有效果，我比较懒，不能坚持下去，喝减肥茶、吃减肥药，可能对身体有副作用。

8.（略）

第十一课　我办了张健身卡

1.（答案合理即可，以下供参考）

房间	肌肉	健康	健身
足球	锻炼	运动	泳池
动感	检查	材料	教练

2.

（1）季卡	（2）流通	（3）减肥	（4）股
（5）定期	（6）室内	（7）恢复	（8）齐全

（9）专业

3.（答案合理即可，以下供参考）

（1）这次表演有专人跳舞。

（2）我们宿舍有专人维修。

（3）动物园的动物各种各样。

（4）朋友的咖啡店开业。

（5）这双鞋子我穿恰好合适。

（6）这家博物馆参观限时120分钟。

4.（答案合理即可，以下供参考）

（1）我家附近恰好有一家健身房开业。

（2）大部分人都选择下班以后去锻炼。

（3）我打算趁着人少的时候去。

（4）我偶尔会闻到一股汗臭味。

（5）健身房有各种各样的健身项目。

（6）我恢复了以前的好身材。

5.（答案合理即可，以下供参考）

（1）高铁确实很方便

（2）偶尔做一次家务

（3）不下雨的话，没问题

（4）没什么事的话

（5）我尽量早点回家

（6）我尽量多和中国人聊天

(7) 我的精神恢复了

(8) 恰好是我想说的

(9) 趁着天没黑

(10) 尽管中文有点难

(11) 早日恢复健康

6. (答案合理即可,以下供参考)

课文 1

(1) 阿里常去的那家健身房,因为她想办一张健身卡。

(2) 季卡,买年卡价格更优惠。

(3) 下午或者晚上晚一点儿,因为这些时候人少,他喜欢人少的时候健身。

(4) 他一般做一些力量练习,偶尔上瑜伽课拉伸肌肉,天气好的话,每周也会游一两次泳。

课文 2

(1) 因为“我”决定健身减肥,同时学校附近恰好有一家健身房刚刚开业。

(2) 比较满意,健身房价格优惠,设施齐全,还有恒温游泳池,健身卡一年两千多元,不限次数,随时可以去,另外,健身房有各种各样的健身项目。

(3) “我”觉得健身的场地有点儿小,人多时空气不流通,会闻到一股汗臭味,让人不舒服;“我”打算以后趁着下午人少的时候去。

7.（答案合理即可，以下供参考）

（1）

a. 游泳　b. 瑜伽　c. 动感单车　d. 健身操

e. 哑铃　f. 杠铃　g. 跑步机　h. 踏板操

i. 划船机

（2）（略）

（3）（略）

8.（略）

第十二课　你看足球比赛吗

1.（答案合理即可，以下供参考）

运动会　电视　比赛　篮球

足球　天气　别人　关注

批评

2.

（1）不管　（2）通常　（3）一连　（4）反正

（5）举办　（6）聚集　（7）尤其　（8）影响

（9）期间

3.（答案合理即可，以下供参考）

（1）昨天我熬夜了，很晚睡觉。

（2）昨天半夜我看篮球比赛直播。

（3）老师上汉字课。

（4）他是一个很特别的学生。

（5）不管遇到什么困难，反正我们都要互相帮助。

（6）不管你们相不相信，反正我相信。

（7）我收到了你的礼物。

（8）班长一分钟一连做了十个动作。

4.（答案合理即可，以下供参考）

（1）足球是全球最有影响力的集体运动。

（2）这个问题受到全国人民的广泛关注。

（3）由于时差，直播时间都在半夜。

（4）不管什么足球比赛，我都喜欢看。

（5）世界杯通常在欧洲或者美洲举办。

5.（答案合理即可，以下供参考）

（1）一连五天下雨

（2）一连吃了十个包子

（3）周末图书馆通常九点开门

（4）反正我去

（5）反正我不相信

（6）受到大家的喜欢

（7）受到老师的批评

（8）尤其对眼睛不好

6.（答案合理即可，以下供参考）

课文 1

（1）因为昨晚熬夜看球赛，今天早上又早起。

（2）世界杯。西班牙对英格兰，西班牙一连踢进三个球，超级精彩，不过，英格兰的守门员也挺厉害的。

（3）C 罗，因为她觉得 C 罗很帅。

课文 2

（1）世界第一运动。因为足球是全球最有影响力的集体运动。

（2）世界杯是每四年举办一届的足球赛事。

（3）晚上不睡觉，很多人聚集在一起熬夜看球。因为世界杯通常在欧洲或者美洲举办，跟中国有时差，比赛直播时间常常在半夜。

7.

（1）（略）

（2）

a. B	b. B	c. A	d. A
e. B	f. B	g. B	h. B

（3）（略）

8.（略）

词汇表 Vocabulary

生词总表（按音序排列）

A

唉*	ài	(10)
安检	ānjiǎn	(6)
安装	ānzhuāng	(4)
按摩	ànmó	(9)
按摩师	ànmó shī	(9)
暗	àn	(2)
熬夜	áoyè	(12)

B

把	bǎ	(6)
摆	bǎi	(7)
班主任	bānzhǔrèn	(2)

注：括号里的数字表示生词所在的课。

Note: The numbers in brackets indicate the lesson where the new words are located.

办理	bànlǐ	(1)
半夜	bànyè	(12)
帮助	bāngzhù	(2)
绑定	bǎng dìng	(1)
包裹	bāoguǒ	(8)
保持	bǎochí	(10)
抱歉*	bàoqiàn	(6)
被	bèi	(8)
比如	bǐrú	(1)
必要	bìyào	(10)
便利	biànlì	(4)
便利店	biànlìdiàn	(1)
冰箱	bīngxiāng	(8)
饼干	bǐnggān	(10)
病历	bìnglì	(3)
不仅……还……	bùjǐn……hái……	(1)
不然	bùrán	(8)
不是……而是……	bú shì……ér shì……	(9)
不小心	bù xiǎoxīn	(2)
不约而同	bùyuē'értóng	(8)

C

材料	cáiliào	(7)
菜谱	càipǔ	(7)

仓库	cāngkù	(8)
尝试	chángshì	(5)
场地	chǎngdì	(11)
超过	chāoguò	(6)
吵	chǎo	(4)
炒	chǎo	(7)
趁着	chèn zhe	(11)
成为	chéngwéi	(1)
成员	chéngyuán	(12)
盛	chéng	(7)
吃货	chīhuò	(10)
充电	chōngdiàn	(6)
充电宝	chōngdiànbǎo	(6)
重新	chóngxīn	(6)
厨房*	chúfáng	(4)
传送带	chuánsòngdài	(6)
窗口	chuāngkǒu	(5)
窗子	chuāngzi	(5)
此外	cǐwài	(8)
次数	cìshù	(11)
葱	cōng	(7)
葱花	cōnghuā	(7)
从……来看	cóng……lái kàn	(9)
促销	cùxiāo	(8)

催	cuī	(9)

D

达人	dárén	(8)
打火机	dǎhuǒjī	(6)
打扫	dǎsǎo	(11)
代替	dàitì	(10)
单车	dānchē	(11)
淡	dàn	(7)
当时	dāngshí	(5)
倒霉	dǎoméi	(3)
到处	dàochù	(8)
到底	dàodǐ	(7)
道	dào	(7)
的话	dehuà	(11)
登机	dēng jī	(6)
登机口	dēng jī kǒu	(6)
登机牌	dēng jī pái	(6)
登录	dēnglù	(9)
等于	děngyú	(7)
地段	dìduàn	(4)
点餐	diǎn cān	(5)
电	diàn	(1)
电池	diànchí	(6)

电商	diànshāng	(8)
定期	dìngqī	(11)
动	dòng	(1)
动手	dòngshǒu	(7)
堆	duī	(8)
剁手*	duò shǒu	(8)

F

发现	fāxiàn	(6)
反正	fǎnzhèng	(12)
方面	fāngmiàn	(9)
房东	fángdōng	(4)
房屋	fángwū	(4)
敷*	fū	(3)
扶	fú	(3)
扶手	fúshǒu	(5)
服药	fúyào	(3)
付款	fù kuǎn	(1)
复杂	fùzá	(7)
副作用	fùzuòyòng	(10)

G

改签	gǎi qiān	(5)

干什么	gàn shénme	(7)
刚好	gānghǎo	(5)
高铁	gāotiě	(5)
高效	gāoxiào	(9)
膏药*	gāoyao	(3)
各	gè	(8)
各种各样	gè zhǒng gè yàng	(11)
更衣室	gēngyīshì	(11)
更不用说	gèng búyòng shuō	(4)
工具	gōngjù	(1)
公里	gōnglǐ	(5)
公寓	gōngyù	(4)
功能	gōngnéng	(1)
攻略	gōnglüè	(8)
购物车	gòu wù chē	(8)
购物节	gòu wù jié	(8)
股	gǔ	(11)
骨头	gǔtou	(3)
骨折	gǔzhé	(3)
关心	guānxīn	(2)
关注	guānzhù	(12)
管	guǎn	(10)
管理	guǎnlǐ	(4)
广播	guǎngbō	(6)
广泛	guǎngfàn	(12)

闺蜜	guīmì	（12）
柜台	guìtái	（6）
贵客	guìkè	（4）
锅	guō	（7）
国际	guójì	（6）

H

害怕	hàipà	（6）
汗臭味	hàn chòu wèi	（11）
航空	hángkōng	（6）
好像	hǎoxiàng	（5）
合租	hézū	（4）
恨不得	hènbude	（2）
恒温	héngwēn	（11）
候车	hòuchē	（5）
候机	hòu jī	（6）
候机室	hòu jī shì	（6）
忽然	hūrán	（6）
糊涂	hútu	（6）
互相	hùxiāng	（2）
话费	huàfèi	（1）
恢复	huīfù	（11）
回国	huí guó	（2）
货比三家	huò bǐ sān jiā	（8）

J

肌肉	jīròu	(11)
鸡蛋液	jī dàn yè	(7)
集体	jítǐ	(12)
技术	jìshù	(1)
季	jì	(11)
加号	jiā hào	(1)
假	jiǎ	(10)
煎饼*	jiānbing	(1)
检查	jiǎnchá	(3)
减	jiǎn	(10)
减肥	jiǎnféi	(10)
简单	jiǎndān	(1)
健康	jiànkāng	(2)
将	jiāng	(9)
角	jiǎo	(1)
脚踝	jiǎo huái	(3)
教练	jiàoliàn	(11)
接着	jiēzhe	(7)
节食	jiéshí	(10)
结果	jiéguǒ	(3)
戒	jiè	(10)
届	jiè	(12)
尽管	jǐnguǎn	(11)

尽量	jǐnliàng	(11)
谨慎	jǐnshèn	(4)
经验	jīngyàn	(8)
景色	jǐngsè	(5)
竟然	jìngrán	(10)
举办	jǔbàn	(12)
举行	jǔxíng	(8)
俱乐部	jùlèbù	(12)
聚集	jùjí	(12)
卷	juǎn	(3)
均衡*	jūnhéng	(10)

K

开业	kāiyè	(11)
靠	kào	(2)
可	kě	(4)
客厅	kètīng	(4)
课间	kèjiān	(2)
空姐	kōngjiě	(6)
空气	kōngqì	(4)
空少	kōng shào	(6)
恐怕	kǒngpà	(10)
控制	kòngzhì	(10)
口服	kǒufú	(3)

口服药	kǒufú yào	(3)
裤脚	kùjiǎo	(3)
快捷	kuàijié	(9)
宽敞	kuānchang	(4)
困难	kùnnan	(2)

L

拉伸	lā shēn	(11)
啦	la	(1)
拦	lán	(6)
懒	lǎn	(9)
浪费	làngfèi	(8)
力量	lìliàng	(11)
立刻	lìkè	(9)
连……也……	lián……yě……	(9)
了不起	liǎobuqǐ	(5)
临时	línshí	(6)
淋浴	línyù	(11)
淋浴间	línyù jiān	(11)
凌晨	língchén	(8)
零钱	língqián	(1)
另外	lìngwài	(5)
另一方面	lìng yì fāngmiàn	(9)
流通	liútōng	(4)

龙虾	lóngxiā	(9)
楼梯	lóutī	(2)
绿色	lǜsè	(7)

M

迈	mài	(10)
慢	màn	(3)
忙碌	mánglù	(8)
毛巾	máojīn	(3)
美称	měichēng	(12)
门铃	ménlíng	(9)
秒	miǎo	(8)
秒杀	miǎoshā	(8)
模糊	móhu	(7)
目前	mùqián	(5)

N

那么	nàme	(7)
难不倒	nán bù dǎo	(7)
扭	niǔ	(3)
弄	nòng	(1)
挪	nuó	(3)

O

偶尔	ǒu'ěr	(11)

P

拍	pāi	(3)
胖	pàng	(10)
配	pèi	(12)
喷雾*	pēn wù	(3)
片子	piānzi	(3)
平方	píngfāng	(4)
平方米	píngfāngmǐ	(4)

Q

期待	qīdài	(9)
期间	qījiān	(12)
齐全	qíquán	(11)
其他	qítā	(1)
其中	qízhōng	(1)
器械	qìxiè	(11)
恰好	qiàhǎo	(11)
钱包	qiánbāo	(1)
墙	qiáng	(3)
切	qiē	(7)

亲爱	qīn'ài	(2)
勤	qín	(10)
球赛	qiúsài	(12)
球员	qiúyuán	(12)
区	qū	(6)
取件	qǔ jiàn	(9)
取票	qǔ piào	(5)
取票机	qǔ piào jī	(5)
取消	qǔxiāo	(6)
去皮	qù pí	(7)
全球	quánqiú	(12)
缺点	quēdiǎn	(9)
确定	quèdìng	(9)
确实	quèshí	(11)

R

热爱	rè'ài	(5)
热量	rèliàng	(10)
人民	rénmín	(12)
肉类	ròu lèi	(9)

S

散	sàn	(7)

伤	shāng	(2)
上门	shàngmén	(9)
稍微	shāowēi	(4)
勺子	sháozi	(7)
少许	shǎoxǔ	(7)
设施	shèshī	(11)
设置	shèzhì	(1)
身材	shēncái	(10)
甚至	shènzhì	(1)
升温	shēngwēn	(10)
生鲜	shēng xiān	(9)
十分	shífēn	(1)
时差	shíchā	(12)
实话	shíhuà	(2)
食品	shípǐn	(9)
世界	shìjiè	(5)
事物	shìwù	(5)
适量	shìliàng	(7)
适应	shìyìng	(2)
室内	shì nèi	(11)
收费	shōu fèi	(11)
手续	shǒuxù	(6)
手艺	shǒuyì	(7)
守门员	shǒuményuán	(12)
首都	shǒudū	(12)

首页	shǒu yè	(1)
受到	shòu dào	(12)
受伤	shòushāng	(2)
瘦	shòu	(5)
蔬菜	shūcài	(9)
摔	shuāi	(2)
帅哥	shuài gē	(12)
水电费	shuǐ diàn fèi	(1)
睡懒觉	shuì lǎnjiào	(4)
顺利	shùnlì	(2)
说实话	shuō shíhuà	(2)
送餐	sòng cān	(5)
送货	sòng huò	(9)
算	suàn	(4)
随便	suíbiàn	(10)
随时	suíshí	(4)
随着	suízhe	(1)

T

摊	tān	(1)
套	tào	(4)
踢	tī	(3)
提	tí	(1)
体重	tǐzhòng	(10)

天呐*	tiān na	(10)
甜食	tiánshí	(10)
挑剔	tiāoti	(4)
调味	tiáowèi	(7)
调味料	tiáowèi liào	(7)
贴	tiē	(3)
厅	tīng	(1)
通常	tōngcháng	(12)
透	tòu	(6)
腿	tuǐ	(10)
退票	tuìpiào	(5)
托运	tuōyùn	(6)

W

完成	wánchéng	(1)
网店	wǎngdiàn	(8)
网费	wǎng fèi	(4)
网站	wǎngzhàn	(5)
未来	wèilái	(9)
闻	wén	(11)
稳	wěn	(5)
问题	wèntí	(3)
蜗牛*	wōniú	(3)
卧室*	wòshì	(4)

无	wú	(9)
无论	wúlùn	(9)
无人	wú rén	(9)
物美价廉	wù měi jià lián	(8)
物业	wùyè	(4)
物业管理费	wùyè guǎnlǐ fèi	(4)

X

下班	xiàbān	(11)
夏装	xiàzhuāng	(10)
先生	xiānsheng	(6)
咸	xián	(7)
现代	xiàndài	(9)
限	xiàn	(11)
相信	xiāngxìn	(10)
箱子	xiāngzi	(6)
响	xiǎng	(9)
消肿	xiāozhǒng	(3)
小哥	xiǎo gē	(8)
小姐	xiǎojiě	(6)
小心	xiǎoxīn	(2)
效果	xiàoguǒ	(10)
心情	xīnqíng	(6)
新闻	xīnwén	(5)

兴奋	xīngfèn	(9)
幸运	xìngyùn	(2)
性价比	xìngjiàbǐ	(8)
许多	xǔduō	(9)

Y

盐	yán	(7)
阳光	yángguāng	(4)
阳台	yángtái	(4)
邀请	yāoqǐng	(4)
舀	yǎo	(7)
药店	yàodiàn	(3)
药房	yàofáng	(3)
液	yè	(7)
一……就……	yī……jiù……	(2)
一连	yìlián	(12)
一切	yíqiè	(2)
医务室	yīwù shì	(2)
咦*	yí	(7)
以内	yǐnèi	(9)
饮食	yǐnshí	(10)
隐私	yǐnsī	(4)
营业	yíngyè	(1)
营业厅	yíngyè tīng	(1)

影响	yǐngxiǎng	(12)
影响力	yǐngxiǎng lì	(12)
应	yìng	(4)
哟*	yō	(2)
用不着	yòng bù zháo	(8)
由于	yóuyú	(6)
有名	yǒumíng	(12)
有氧运动	yǒuyǎng yùndòng	(10)
于是	yúshì	(7)
遇到	yù dào	(2)

Z

早日	zǎorì	(11)
宅女	zháinǚ	(10)
照顾	zhàogù	(2)
照相机	zhàoxiàngjī	(6)
正常	zhèngcháng	(3)
正门	zhèngmén	(4)
直播	zhíbō	(12)
值得	zhídé	(1)
值得一提	zhídé yì tí	(1)
只有……才……	zhǐyǒu……cái……	(8)
智能化	zhìnéng huà	(9)
至少	zhìshǎo	(10)

中介	zhōngjiè	(4)
终于	zhōngyú	(10)
肿	zhǒng	(3)
周围	zhōuwéi	(4)
主食	zhǔshí	(10)
专人	zhuānrén	(11)
转账	zhuǎnzhàng	(1)
准时	zhǔnshí	(5)
走动	zǒudòng	(3)
走廊	zǒuláng	(5)
走路	zǒulù	(3)
租	zū	(4)
租金	zūjīn	(4)
嘴	zuǐ	(10)
做法	zuòfǎ	(7)

专名

澳大利亚*	Àodàlìyà	(9)
C 罗*	C Luó	(12)
德甲*	Dé jiǎ	(12)
动感单车	Dònggǎn dānchē	(11)
荷兰*	Hélán	(9)
黑色星期五	Hēisè xīngqī wǔ	(8)
皇家马德里*	Huángjiā Mǎdélǐ	(12)
马德里*	Mǎdélǐ	(12)

美洲	Měizhōu	(12)
欧冠*	Ōu Guàn	(12)
欧洲	Ōuzhōu	(12)
葡萄牙*	Pútáoyá	(12)
深圳*	Shēnzhèn	(5)
世界杯	Shìjiè bēi	(12)
双十一	Shuāng shíyī	(8)
泰国*	Tàiguó	(9)
天猫	Tiānmāo	(8)
西甲*	Xī Jiǎ	(12)
新西兰*	Xīnxīlán	(9)
意甲*	Yì Jiǎ	(12)
英超*	Yīng Chāo	(12)
英格兰*	Yīnggélán	(12)
中国南方航空*	Zhōngguó nánfāng hángkōng	(6)

MPR 出版物链码使用说明

本书中凡文字下方带有链码图标“══”的地方，均可通过“泛媒关联”App 的扫码功能或“泛媒阅读”App 的“扫一扫”功能，获得对应的多媒体内容。

您可以通过扫描下方的二维码下载“泛媒关联”App、“泛媒阅读”App。

“泛媒关联”App 链码扫描操作步骤：

1. 打开“泛媒关联”App；
2. 将扫码框对准书中的链码扫描，即可播放多媒体内容。

“泛媒阅读”App 链码扫描操作步骤：

1. 打开“泛媒阅读”App；
2. 打开“扫一扫”功能；
3. 扫描书中的链码，即可播放多媒体内容。

扫码体验：